Reconceptualising Maths and Science Teaching and Learning

Edited by:

Stephen Dinham
Russell Tytler
Deborah Corrigan
David Hoxley

Published in 2025 by Amba Press, Melbourne, Australia
www.ambapress.com.au

First published in 2018 by ACER Press, an imprint of
Australian Council for Educational Research Ltd

© Stephen Dinham, Russell Tytler, Deborah Corrigan, David Hoxley (Editors) 2025

This book is copyright. All rights reserved. Except under the conditions described in the Copyright Act 1968 of Australia and subsequent amendments, and any exceptions permitted under the current statutory licence scheme administered by Copyright Agency (www.copyright.com.au), no part of this publication may be reproduced, stored in a retrieval system, transmitted, broadcast or communicated in any form or by any means, optical, digital, electronic, mechanical, photocopying, recording or otherwise, without the written permission of the publisher.

Cover design, text design and typesetting by Peter Long.
Cover image © Hero Images Inc. / Alamy Stock Photo

ISBN: 9781923569362 (pbk)
ISBN: 9781923569379 (ebk)

A catalogue record for this book is available from the National Library of Australia.

Contents

Acronyms	*viii*
Acknowledgments	*x*
List of tables and figures	*xviii*

Part A—Issues of mathematics and science teaching and teacher education: Background to ReMSTEP — 1

Chapter 1: Responding to concerns about mathematics and science education — 2

- The dimensions of the challenge — 3
- Aligning school mathematics and science with professional disciplinary practice — 9
- Conclusion — 11
- *Implications for PST education in mathematics and science* — 11

Chapter 2: Background and overview of ReMSTEP — 13

- The overarching program: Enhancing the training of mathematics and science teachers — 13
- The projects comprising the ETMST program — 16
- Conclusion — 17

Chapter 3: Key innovations and methodology of ReMSTEP — 19

Introduction and context to ReMSTEP — 19
- *Typical responses* — 21
- *The need for reconceptualisation* — 22
- Details of ReMSTEP — 23
- Nature of the sites and collaborative practices — 26
- The innovations — 28
- Integrating cutting-edge practices and pedagogy — 29
  - *A focus on practice rather than knowledge* — 29
  - *Inquiry, problem solving, modelling, context* — 30

Project infrastructure and management — 32

Parts B and C — 32

Part B—ReMSTEP: The innovations — 33

Review — 34
- Introduction — 34
- The innovations — 37
- Conclusion — 43

Chapter 4: *Innovation 1*—Contemporary mathematics and science integrated into PSTs' units of study — 45
- Introduction — 45
- Engaging in practices of contemporary sciences — 46
  - *Evaluating the innovation* — 52
  - *Results* — 53
  - *Conclusions* — 55
- Creation of mathematics teaching videos — 56
  - *Approach to evaluation* — 58
- Conclusion — 60

Chapter 5: *Innovation 2*—Science students in schools — 61
- Introduction — 61
- A portfolio of approaches — 63
  - *Schools Science Project* — 64
  - *Back to School* — 66
  - *Science in Schools* — 67
- Outcomes — 68
- Conclusion — 74

Chapter 6: *Innovation 3*—Mathematics and science teaching specialisations within primary pre-service teaching programs — 76
- Introduction — 76
  - The activities — 78
    - *Science and mathematics specialist pathways in Master of Teaching (Primary)* — 79

Multidisciplinary Science and Technology Integrated Experience	84
Conclusion	89

Chapter 7: *Innovation 4*—Specialist science and technology centre collaborations — 90

Introduction	90
Gene Technology Access Centre	91
Discovery Science and Technology Centre	91
Melbourne Museum	92
Reconceptualising Rocks	93
The activity	94
Impacts of the activity	97
Collaboration and networks/partnerships: Making them work	103
Conclusion	106
Key learnings from the ReMSTEP specialist science centre partnerships	106

Chapter 8: *Innovation 5*—Exploring models of interaction between scientists and PSTs — 108

Introduction	108
Exploring models of interaction	112
Narrative examples: Four interactions	114
Stem cell exploration	114
Multimedia resources for biology and environmental education	116
Institute of Frontier Materials (IFM) research practices video-supported activity modules	120
Contemporary Science Workshops	124
Findings and discussion	127
Findings regarding outcomes	130
Challenges for models of interaction	131
What have we learned?	133
Conclusion	134
What remains to be learned? What are possible ways forward?	134

Chapter 9: *Innovations 6 & 7*—Building the pipeline: Recruiting high-potential mathematics and science teachers and leveraging existing student expertise 136

    Introduction 136

    Innovation 7: Building a recruitment pipeline of high-potential mathematics and science teachers 137

        Schools Science Project 138

        AMSPP partnerships: ASELL, GTP, FARLabs and In2science 139

        Science Students in Schools 142

    Innovation 6: Building on existing student expertise in mathematics and science 143

        Back to School 143

        Communicating Science 145

    Conclusion 146

Part C—Findings and implications of the project 149

    Introduction 150

Chapter 10: Overall findings of ReMSTEP 152

    Introduction 152

    The project approach 152

    ReMSTEP impact 156

    Collaborations and networks 156

        STEM researchers and agencies 156

        Cross-faculty collaboration 159

        Interaction with local schools 162

    Impacts on PSTs 165

        New knowledge and skills 165

        Shifted perceptions and attitude 167

        Improved confidence and capacity 172

    Impact on tertiary mathematics and science students 175

Chapter 11: Conclusions and implications ... 179
    The role of collaboration ... 179
    STEM and STEM education ... 180
    Implications and recommendations ... 184

Appendices ... 188
    Appendix 1: Overview of ReMSTEP achievements ... 188
    Appendix 2: ReMSTEP connections ... 189
    Appendix 3: The ReMSTEP Program logic ... 190
    Appendix 4: Interview questions used during evaluation ... 191
    Appendix 5: Sample survey questions used during evaluation ... 194

References ... 196

Acronyms

AITSL	Australian Institute for Teaching and School Leadership
ARC	Australian Research Council
ASELL	Advancing Science by Enhancing Learning in the Laboratory
AMSPP	Australian Mathematics & Science Partnership Program
BSc	Bachelor of Science
CADET	Centre for Advanced Design in Engineering Training
CSIRO	Commonwealth Scientific and Industrial Research Organisation
DEECD	Department of Education and Early Childhood Development
DET	Department of Education and Training
ETMST	Enhancing the Training of Mathematics and Science Teachers
FARLabs	Freely Accessible Remote Laboratories
GTAC	The Gene Technology Access Centre
GTP	Growing Tall Poppies
ICT	Information and Communication Technologies
IFM	Institute for Frontier Materials
MSS	Monash Science Squad
MSTE	Multidisciplinary Science and Technology in Education
MTeach	Master of Teaching
NESB	Non-English-speaking background

NoS	Nature of Sciences
OECD	Organisation for Economic Co-operation and Development
OLT	Office for Learning and Teaching
PISA	Programme for International Student Assessment
PST	Pre-service teacher
ReMSTEP	Reconceptualising Mathematics and Science Teacher Education Programs
R&D	Research and development
SCTE	School Centres for Teaching Excellence
SES	Socio-economic status
SiAS	Staff in Australia's Schools
SMiS	Scientists and Mathematicians in Schools
SPiES	Scientists as Partners in Education
STAV	Science Teachers Association of Victoria
STEM	Science, technology, engineering and mathematics
TIMSS	Trends in International Mathematics and Science Study
TSA	Tertiary student assistant
VCE	Victorian Certificate of Education
VSSEC	Victorian Space Science Education Centre

Acknowledgments

Lead institution

The University of Melbourne

Partner institutions

Deakin University
La Trobe University
Monash University

Chief investigators

- Stephen Dinham: Professor, Melbourne Graduate School of Education, The University of Melbourne [Project leader and Editor]

- David Clarke: Professor, Melbourne Graduate School of Education, The University of Melbourne

- Deborah Corrigan: Professor, Centre for Science, Mathematics and Technology Education, Faculty of Education, Monash University [Editor]

- David Hoxley: Lecturer, La Trobe Institute for Molecular Science, Department of Chemistry and Physics, La Trobe University, Bundoora [Editor]

- Michelle Livett: Associate Professor, School of Physics, The University of Melbourne

- Stuart Palmer: Associate Professor, Faculty of Science, Engineering and Built Environment, Deakin University, Geelong

- Vaughan Prain: Professor in Science Interdisciplinary Education Research, Faculty of Arts and Education, Deakin University, Geelong (formerly La Trobe University at the commencement of ReMSTEP)
- Russell Tytler: Alfred Deakin Professor and Chair in Science Education, Faculty of Arts and Education, Deakin University, Burwood [Editor]
- Cristina Varsavsky: Professor, School of Mathematical Sciences, Monash University

Team members

- Dr Joanne Burke, Project Officer, Monash University
- Ms Lisa Fazio, Project Officer, Monash University
- Dr Leissa Kelly, Project Officer, Deakin University
- Daniel Nicholls, Project Manager
- Albert Penticoss, Web Designer
- Nick Tran, Project Officer, La Trobe University
- Dr Yuan Gao, Evaluation Officer

Chapter authors

Dr Melody Anderson: Senior Lecturer, Melbourne Graduate School of Education, The University of Melbourne

Dr Joanne Burke: Project Officer, Centre for Science, Mathematics and Technology Education, Faculty of Education, Monash University

Dr Rebecca Cooper: Lecturer, Faculty of Education, Monash University

Dr Peter Cox: Lecturer, Department of Education, College of Arts, Social Sciences and Commerce, La Trobe University, Bendigo

Dr Norman Do: Lecturer, School of Mathematical Sciences, Monash University

Maria Gibson: Senior Lecturer Emeritus, School of Life and Environmental Sciences, Deakin University, Burwood

Dr Leissa Kelly: Project Officer, Deakin University, Melbourne

Mr Greg Lancaster: Lecturer, Faculty of Education, Monash University

Michelle Livett: Associate Professor, School of Physics, The University of Melbourne

Mr David Overton: Lecturer, School of Chemistry, Monash University

Stuart Palmer: Associate Professor, Faculty of Science Engineering and the Built Environment, Deakin University, Geelong

Dr Rannah Scamporlino: Director of Learning, Education 121 Learning Centre

Wee Tiong Seah: Associate Professor, Melbourne Graduate School of Education, The University of Melbourne

Dr James Stratford: Project Officer, La Trobe Institute for Molecular Science, Department of Chemistry and Physics, La Trobe University, Bundoora

Nick Tran: Project Officer, Lecturer, Department of Education, College of Arts, Social Sciences and Commerce, La Trobe University, Bendigo

Dr Kelly-Anne Twist: Project Officer, Affiliation, Centre for Science, Mathematics and Technology Education, Faculty of Education, Monash University

Cristina Varsavsky: Professor, School of Mathematical Sciences, Monash University

Peta White: Lecturer, Faculty of Arts and Education, Deakin University, Burwood

The following people also made valuable contributions to this project:

Aurelie Abel
Professor Peter Aubusson, University of Technology Sydney
Professor Leigh Ackland, Deakin University
Dr Ben Allardyce, Deakin University
Ms Denise Athanasopoulos, Monash University
Nicole Banko, Deakin University
Elke Barczak, Museum Victoria
Dr Eroia Barone-Nugent, The University of Melbourne
Professor Bill Barton, Auckland University
Stephanie Beames, The University of Queensland
Kathleen Beggs, Deakin University
Rachael Begley
Ian Bentley, Deakin University
Luca Bertolacci, Victorian Space Science Education Centre
Lou Bowe, Whole School Partners
Peter Bowman, The University of Melbourne
Alise Brown, Deakin University
Dr Damien Callahan, Deakin University
Tamara Camilleri, Deakin University
Geraldine Carrol (ex-Project Manager)
Dr Michael Cater, Deakin University
Ann Cathcart
Cornelia Cefai
Associate Professor Helen Chick, University of Tasmania
Dr Gail Chittleborough, Deakin University
Connie Cirkony, Deakin University
Adam Cole
Leanne Collins
Dr Xavier Conlan, Deakin University
Rebecca Connors, Deakin University
Associate Professor Paul Corcoran, University of South Australia
Dr Mary Coupland, University of Tasmania

Dr John Cripps Clark, Deakin University
Dr Merryn Dawborn-Gundlach, The University of Melbourne
Professor Les Dawes, Queensland University of Technology
Dr Mandy De Souza, IFM
Discovery Science and Technology Centre, Bendigo
DO Consulting
Dr Madeleine Dupont, IFM
Jacinta Duncan, GTAC
Gavin Edwards, Victorian DET
Professor Maria Forsyth, IFM
Professor Browyn Fox, IFM
Priscilla Gaff, Museum Victoria
Dr Yuan Gao, The University of Melbourne
Gene Technology Access Centre
Dr Maria Gibson, Deakin University
Shannon Gleeson, Deakin University
Glenn Dixon Visuals
Associate Professor Susie Groves, Deakin University
Dr Matthew Hall, Monash University
Kathleen Hayes, Deakin University
Dr Dermot Henry, Museum Victoria
Dr Rannah Hetherington, The University of Melbourne
Dr Matthias Hilder, IFM
Associate Professor Linda Hobbs, Deakin University
Nicole Holton, Deakin University
Amy Hooper
Associate Professor Peter Hubber, Deakin University
In2science
Dr Simon James, Deakin University
Dan Jazby, The University of Melbourne
Dr Gayle Jenkins, Deakin University
Dr Matt Jennings, IFM
Jenny Jerbic, Deakin University
Dr Tim Jessop, Deakin University

Dr Wendy Jobling, Deakin University
Dr Tim Johns, La Trobe University
Owen Kaluza, Monash University
Dr Vinay Shekhar Kandagal, IFM
Dr Zohreh Keshavarz, IFM
Associate Professor Gillian Kidman, Monash University
Associate Professor Deborah King, The University of Melbourne
Kylie Koulkoudinas, Deakin University
Nina Levin, Deakin University
Dr Chris Lim, Deakin University
Associate Professor Kieran Lim, Deakin University
Jennifer Ling
Dr Benjamin Long, Deakin University
Dr John Long, Deakin University
Scott Mackenzie
Magnolia Lowe Film Communications
Faezeh Makhlooghiazad, IFM
Tom McCann, Deakin University
Jorja McKinnon, Deakin University
Kate McLaughlin, Deakin University
Professor Joanne Mulligan, Macquarie University
Museum Victoria
Dr Maryam Naebe, IFM
Sophie Nakos
Tim Newport, The University of Melbourne
Annie Nguyen, The University of Melbourne
Melissa Nugent, Queensland University of Technology
Graeme Oliver, La Trobe University
Anastasia Parker, Deakin University
Krystle Perdevski
Jenny Pesina (ex-Learning Designer)
Amanda Peters, Deakin University
Bettina Pfaendner, The University of Melbourne
Louisa Phillipson

Barry Plant, Deakin University
Dr Nicholas Porch, Deakin University
Dr Jenny Pringle, IFM
Quantum Victoria
Dr Jo Raphael, Deakin University
Ryan Raybould, Deakin University
Dr Christine Redman, The University of Melbourne
Oliver Reeve
Professor John Rice, ACDS
Dr Euan Ritchie, Deakin University
Dr Lee Rollins, Deakin University
Dr Elise Roper, Deakin University
Sarah Rosen
Christine Sang
Dr Aaron Schultz, Deakin University
Amanda Scott, Southern Cross University
Associate Professor Wee Tiong Seah, The University of Melbourne
Professor Guang Shi, Deakin University
Kathryn Sobey
Anna Sutjiadi, Monash University
Duncan Symons, The University of Melbourne
Jim Tangas, Victorian DET
Professor Roy Tasker
Glen Toohey, Department of Education
Damian Toussaint
Fiona Trapani, The University of Melbourne
Tracey Tsang, Deakin University
Dr Kelly-Anne Twist, Monash University
Mary Vamvakas
Dr Sanya Van Huet, Deakin University
Victoria Space Science Education Centre
Miranda Waddick, Deakin University
Di Walsh
Professor Xungai Wang, IFM

Anna Watts, Deakin University
Dr Matthias Weiss, IFM
Michael Westcott, Deakin University
Dr David Williams, Deakin University
Dr Gaye Williams, Deakin University
Greg Williamson
Alysia Wood-Bradley
Andrew Wright, Deakin University
Esme Wright, Deakin University
Dr Jane Wright
Dr Ruhamah Yunis, IFM
Yundong Zhou, IFM

Particular thanks to all the university students who participated in the project. Thank you to all the primary and secondary schools that collaborated on the project. Michaela Skelly provided editorial support for the production of this book.

Support for the production of this publication has been provided by the Australian Government Department of Education and Training. The views expressed in this publication do not necessarily reflect the views of the Australian Government Department of Education and Training.

List of tables and figures

TABLE 4.1 Schema for science cognitive engagement

TABLE 5.1 Three models for engaging tertiary science students with schools

TABLE 6.1 Average Likert responses to survey questions with indicative quotes

TABLE 8.1 The percentage of 'agree' and 'strongly agree' responses to three key questions from 2016 online surveys

TABLE 10.1 Number of tertiary students involved in ReMSTEP activities

FIGURE 6.1 Year 1 Girton Grammar student exploring borax crystals they grew under the direction of a synchrotron scientist

FIGURE 7.1 a. Melbourne Museum research scientist showing students samples collected on recent fieldtrips; b. Melbourne Museum research scientist, Dr David Pickering, discusses a recent discovery of dinosaur bones and the impact this had on understanding the species' physiology

FIGURE 7.2 Reconceptualising Rocks, Phillip Island field trip

FIGURE 7.3 a. A geologist pointing out rock formations in roadside cuttings; b. Students exploring 'The Giant's Steps' at Organ Pipes National Park with a geologist

FIGURE 8.1 A generalised model of interactions under *Innovation 5* activities

FIGURE 8.2 The storyboard for developing the multimedia explanation

FIGURE 8.3 An example of a multimedia resource; several multimedia explanations have been presented

FIGURE 8.4 Resource production models for the *Innovation 5* activities

Part A

Issues of mathematics and science teaching and teacher education: Background to ReMSTEP

Chapter 1

Responding to concerns about mathematics and science education

Russell Tytler, Stephen Dinham, Deborah Corrigan, David Hoxley

Concerns about mathematics and science education are widely canvassed and well documented at policy level in Australia[1] and in numerous countries internationally[2]. In Australia, there is increasing concern at declining participation in advanced level school mathematics and physical sciences, fewer students electing to study particular science, technology, engineering and mathematics (STEM) programs at university[3], and evidence of Australian students' declining performance on comparative international tests in mathematics and science[4] (these matters are discussed in more detail later in this section). There is also mounting concern that school mathematics and science are failing to help students develop the problem-solving and critical reasoning skills that will prepare them to tackle the challenges entailed in generating productive futures for themselves and, more generally, enhancing national wealth[5]. In response to these concerns, government agencies and school systems have been promoting the need for new ways of teaching the STEM subjects, with particular reference to mathematics and science[6].

---

1   Office of the Chief Scientist 2012a; 2014; 2016
2   Freeman et al. 2015; Marginson et al. 2013; Tytler 2007
3   Freeman et al. 2015
4   Thomson et al. 2016
5   Australian Government 2016; National Council 2015
6   National Council 2015; Office of the Chief Scientist 2016

The constructs of mathematical and scientific literacy, increasingly referred to in curriculum frameworks globally, emphasise the need for students, and not simply a STEM elite, to develop knowledge, skills and positive dispositions in these core subjects[7]. Yet, particularly in technologically advanced societies, there is evidence that many students develop increasingly negative attitudes to school mathematics and science across the primary and early secondary school years[8]. Student engagement with mathematics and science, and the development of dispositions towards STEM knowledge and perspectives more generally, is thus an increasing focus[9]. In recent reports in Australia, there has been a strong recognition of the importance of STEM thinking and skills for all students and an advocacy of the need to bring school mathematics and science closer to the way mathematics and science are practised in contemporary settings[10].

Recently, the Australian government has provided substantial funding, which has led to a flurry of STEM activity in schools, school jurisdictions and universities, with little cohesion between the activities. A STEM Education Forum was held in Sydney in 2015 with a representative group of key stakeholders to develop a National STEM School Education Strategy, 2016–26[11]. Chief among the key areas identified for national action was the need to increase student STEM ability, engagement, participation and aspiration; and to increase teacher capacity and STEM teaching quality.

The dimensions of the challenge

Research into school mathematics and science focusing on the underlying issues identified above, indicates a number of interacting dimensions to the problem. These relate to socio-economic issues, to teacher supply, to teacher knowledge and confidence, and to traditional teaching and

---

7   Bybee 1997; Stacey 2010; Tytler & Symington 2006
8   Boaler 1997; Goodrum et al. 2001, Nardi & Steward 2003; Tytler & Osborne 2012
9   Breiner et al. 2012; Hackling et al. 2013; Honey et al. 2014; Tytler 2007
10 Hackling et al. 2013; Office of the Chief Scientist 2012a
11 National Council 2015

learning approaches. We will discuss these in turn.

Student achievement in mathematics and science and their attitudes to these subjects have strong socio-economic correlates. For instance, students from higher socio-economic levels are disproportionately represented in enrolments in post-compulsory physical sciences[12]. Evidence indicates this is related not so much to economic factors but to the cultural capital particularly provided by higher socio-economic groupings, and groups for which education and STEM education is particularly highly valued[13]. Parental expectations and parental support have been identified as important factors in determining participation in STEM pathways[14]. Lyons[15] found that students with a parent or relative who worked in STEM areas were more likely to choose physical science and higher mathematics subjects (which were seen as difficult, with delayed rewards). This relates in part to whether students are exposed to information about potential STEM career pathways, and there is evidence that at all levels of schooling[16], lack of knowledge of careers and misinformation about where STEM subjects can lead are negative influences when selecting post-compulsory mathematics and science.

Further to this, there are strong positive influences associated with students' exposure to professionals of the scientific and mathematical communities. There is growing understanding that choice of school subjects is fundamentally an identity choice, such that students, if they are to follow a STEM pathway, need to develop an identity that is consistent with their concept of what it is to be a practising mathematician or scientist[17]. This is a particularly cogent issue with girls and STEM choices, where role models and expectations from teachers, parents and curriculum framing often represent a strong

---

12   Lyons 2006b
13   Archer et al. 2007
14   Archer et al. 2007
15   Lyons 2006b
16   Lindahl 2007
17   Tytler 2014

gender bias[18]. Identity is also a powerful lens through which to understand issues around Indigenous participation in STEM pathways, with Indigenous students needing to learn to 'border cross' into a scientific perspective that may be at odds with traditional Indigenous epistemologies and expectations[19]. The identity issue, while particularly powerful for understanding gender and Indigenous responses to science, is an important construct to understand more generally the difficulties students face engaging with school science, since for most students it represents a cultural imposition with its specialist epistemologies and associated language forms. Thus, it is important, if students are to develop positive dispositions towards futures in school mathematics and science, that they have access to positive role models representing what it is to think and work scientifically and mathematically. These role models may be parents, enthusiastic teachers[20], or other STEM professionals they interact with informally or through school programs[21].

Stuckey[22] and colleagues have defined 'relevance' in science education as an issue. They contend that 'science learning becomes relevant education whenever learning will have (positive) consequences for the student's life'. In this instance, positive consequences can include fulfilling students' current and future personal interests and educational demands and expectations. In much the same way that values include internal and external sociological values, Stuckey and colleagues insist that relevance in science education covers both intrinsic components such as students' interests and motives, and extrinsic components such as 'ethically justified expectations of one's personal environment and the society in which they operate and live'. From this perspective, relevance in science education comprises three dimensions: individual, societal and vocational. Such a view of

---

18   Adamuti-Trache & Andres 2007
19   Aikenhead 2001; 2013
20   Darby 2005
21   Tytler et al. 2015
22   Stuckey et al. 2013, pp. 19–20

relevance links well when considering values—the guiding principles individuals choose to live by. Learning mathematics and science and whether students perceive such learning as relevant, will depend on how well we can promote the values that underpin such education to learners in ways that provide positive consequences for their lives. Aligning the values of science education with a student's personal values is often not considered, as evidenced in previous iterations of science curricula with its emphasis on what has become known as 'canonical science'[23].

An issue that is becoming increasingly recognised in Australia, particularly in rural areas, is the shortage of mathematics and science teachers, and the increasing incidence of mathematics and science classes being taken by teachers not fully qualified in these disciplines. The problem is difficult to quantify because of lack of agreement on what constitutes a teacher who is 'out-of-field'. A 2011 study found that in Years 7–10 mathematics, only 62 per cent of teachers had two or more years' tertiary mathematics (the minimum required to teach mathematics in most countries). More than one-third, 39 per cent, were teaching out-of-field, and 23 per cent had not studied tertiary mathematics at all[24]. The evidence on the relationship between teacher qualifications and student learning is complex, and there is evidence that depending on their adaptability, under-qualified teachers can be very successful in supporting learning[25]. However, there is also evidence that teachers need deep and flexible knowledge if they are to support students in the problem solving and critical reasoning Australia needs to aspire to[26]. There is an urgent need to attract capable students of mathematics and science into teacher education to overcome present teacher shortages.

Associated with this out-of-field problem in secondary schools is the problem that some primary teachers may not have taken university, or

---

23 Aikenhead 2006
24 Marginson et al. 2013
25 Hobbs 2012
26 Fennema & Franke 1992

even final year secondary mathematics and science subjects. There has been a history of research into primary teachers' lack of confidence and competence in mathematics and science[27], and for science a history of research studies shows a disturbing lack of curriculum time devoted to primary science[28], although the degree to which science is integrated into other subjects and topics is uncertain and no doubt variable. The Victorian government has, with some success, instituted a program of training specialist teachers of mathematics and science who are trained in subject matter knowledge, pedagogy and leadership; tasked with leading innovation in these subjects in the schools, supporting other teachers with planning and implementing changed curriculum[29]. There are calls for instituting, as part of teacher education, specialist options whereby pre-service teachers (PSTs) can elect to focus on subject areas of interest to them, with the expectation they could provide support in primary schools for other teachers to plan and implement STEM curriculum experiences.[30]

Research into student attitudes across the primary and early secondary school years shows a general decrease in positive attitudes, particularly in early secondary school. Students' decisions about whether to continue with STEM subjects occurs earlier than hitherto thought, as early as in the mid-primary school years and well before the age of 13[31]. This has led to increased government focus and investment in STEM education in the primary and early secondary years.

In addition to the issues of socio-economic and identity factors, and teacher supply and quality described above, a major factor in these attitudinal issues is the adherence to traditional teaching and learning practices, which are based on a knowledge-delivery recall model that

---

27 Tytler 2007; Committee for the Review of Teaching and Teacher Education 2003
28 Goodrum et al. 2001
29 Campbell & Chittleborough 2014
30 The 2014 Teacher Education Ministerial Advisory Group (TEMAG) called for such primary specialisations to be introduced into initial teacher education programs. Teacher Education Ministerial Advisory Group 2014
31 Tytler et al. 2008

fails to engage students in varied activities and opportunities to be challenged to explore and generate ideas[32]. Students often complain about the lack of personal relevance of traditional mathematics and science curricula. Lindahl[33] found that her Swedish upper-primary school students resented the lack of opportunity for personal opinion and expression in science, caused by the narrow range of transmissive pedagogies used. Osbourne and Collins[34] UK informants talked of the prevalence of closed questions with 'right or wrong answers' with no time, in the rush to ingest concepts, to discuss or reflect or offer opinions. Lyons'[35] meta-analysis of the findings of a number of interview studies identified three major themes: the transmissive pedagogy characterising school science; the decontextualised content that fails to engage students' interest or commitment; and the unnecessary difficulty of school science. However, there are 'pockets' of change. For example, Loughran and Smith[36] document changed practice in both primary and secondary teachers when teaching science as a result of a sustained professional learning.

Researchers have found a similar picture for mathematics. Many mathematics classes in Australia do not require thinking beyond simple analysis[37], which means that the intellectual quality of mathematics learning is often minimal. In mathematics classes where students mainly memorise and repeat rules and procedures, rather than explore to develop mathematical ideas, they lack control over their learning, leading to a similar disengagement as that for science. Many mathematics educators advocate greater use of authentic tasks in mathematics—tasks containing 'real-world' contexts that are meaningful to the students and that are likely to engage them in actively exploring associated mathematics[38].

---

32   Tytler & Osborne 2012
33   Lindahl 2007
34   Osbourne & Collins 2001
35   Lyons 2006a
36   Loughran & Smith 2015
37   Wood et al. 2006
38   e.g. Galbraith 2006a; Galbraith et al. 2006; Howard & Perry 2007

Aligning school mathematics and science with professional disciplinary practice

This focus on authentic tasks underpins current advocacy of integrated STEM activities and curricula where mathematics and science are taught within interdisciplinary settings often involving engineering design and digital technologies[39]. A major US report raised questions about the depth of learning in mathematics and science that ensues from such interrelated activities[40]. However, there is ongoing enthusiasm for exploring interdisciplinary STEM models on the basis that such activities bring school mathematics and science closer to authentic professional practice in the disciplines, and engage students in ways that traditional single-subject curricular approaches do not.

Allied to this advocacy of authentic or real-world tasks, is increasing interest in and advocacy of having the school mathematics and science curriculum better reflect the professional knowledge-building practices in these disciplines. Providing opportunities for students to engage in such tasks allows them to engage in contemporary mathematical and scientific problem-solving practices, rather than more traditional, highly stylised practices that are less relevant. In both mathematics and science, part of this advocacy revolves around defining inquiry approaches to better reflect the increasing recognition that both scientific discovery and mathematics knowledge construction are built around inventing representational systems that enable new ways of seeing. Latour[41] argued that the emergence of scientific thought depends on developing representational tools or 'inscriptions' that can be combined, transformed across modes (including being turned into figures or supported by writing), and reproduced. Mathematics and science education researchers are working with teachers to develop approaches to school mathematics and science that focus on introducing students to the material and

---

39 English 2016; Vasquez 2015
40 Honey et al. 2014
41 Latour 1986, p. 3

representational practices through which knowledge is built and communicated[42].

However, it is not only the representational practices that are important, but also the communication of such practices and knowledge to a variety of audiences, including the general public. The ability to tell and generate responses to authentic stories about science requires an interactive contextual process as the recipient deconstructs and reconstructs the story into a form that is useful to their personal needs and circumstances[43].

Further to this advocacy of bringing school mathematics and science closer to authentic disciplinary practices, there is increased interest at the policy level in involving STEM professionals in direct interactions with schools and students[44]. There have been a number of initiatives mapping school-community science partnerships, and researchers have explored the experience and outcomes of a range of such initiatives, where schools have formed partnerships with members of the scientific community, often local, to provide support for innovative science curricula.[45] Such activities have led to enhanced student outcomes, and often more progressive, student-centred pedagogies. Since 2007, the Commonwealth Scientific and Industrial Research Organisation (CSIRO) runs Scientists and Mathematicians in Schools (SMiS), a national program supporting partnerships between teachers and mathematics and science professionals, which has generated more than 4600 partnerships . An evaluation of the SMiS program showed evidence of significant student outcomes including:

> … increasing engagement with science, mathematics and ICT learning and reasoning, increased interest and enjoyment and knowledge and confidence in STEM subjects, awareness of how scientists and mathematicians think and work, increased appreciation of STEM

---

42 Prain & Tytler 2012; Tytler et al. 2013; Lehrer & Schauble 2000; 2002
43 Rennie 2007
44 Office of the Chief Scientist 2012a; Australian Government 2016
45 Tytler et al. 2011; 2016

professionals as people, and knowledge of and enhanced attitudes towards, STEM pathways and careers.[46]

The partnerships under SMiS provided significant opportunities to explore the 'inquiry', 'reasoning' and 'problem solving' and 'science as a human endeavour' strands of the Australian mathematics and science curricula. The mathematicians and scientists bring to schools their knowledge and dispositions, their passion and curiosity, their capacity to exemplify and tell stories about what it is to work in STEM and how such knowledge is built. These findings are all consistent with what we know about how STEM-aligned identity is developed[47]. The evaluation found that the most effective partnerships were built around joint planning and a developing mutual regard between STEM professionals and teachers for their respective expertise. STEM professionals did not expect or manage to solve the problems of STEM education on their own, but did so in partnership with teachers.

Conclusion

Implications for PST education in mathematics and science

In line with the reform of mathematics and science curricular practices implied by the developing ideas described earlier, there is a clear need to rethink our traditional mathematics and science teacher education practices. In particular, the project Reconceptualising Mathematics and Science Teacher Education Programs (ReMSTEP) took as its brief within the Enhancing the Training of Mathematics and Sciences Teachers (ETMST) program (see Chapter 2) the need to prepare graduates who can act as change agents to make mathematics and science curricula more engaging, challenging and relevant for students. The approach taken by ReMSTEP responded to the following curricular and teacher education directions informed by the ideas described on page 12:

---

46 Tytler et al. 2015, p. 8
47 Tytler 2014

1. Inclusion in the curriculum of information and role models showing the relevance of STEM knowledge and skills to productive futures—how mathematics and science work in the world.

2. A focus on problem solving and critical reasoning where students engage with contemporary mathematics and science knowledge building practices in response to authentic and meaningful challenges.

3. Recruiting more mathematics and science teachers, particularly those who are capable of leading innovation in schools. This includes mathematics and science specialists for primary schools, and teachers with strong disciplinary capabilities in secondary schools capable of productive partnerships with the professional STEM community.

4. The encouragement of partnerships between schools and the STEM community and the development of curricular approaches that will make best use of STEM professionals' knowledge, skills and dispositions.

Following this, the 'reconceptualising' offered by ReMSTEP involves forging and sustaining direct links between the professional science and mathematics communities and the education communities, in order to introduce teacher education students to experiences, curricular activities and exemplar resources, which better represent the contemporary practice of mathematics and science. Through this process, we can enhance school students' identities, conceptions and capabilities in science and mathematics.

The following chapters go into greater detail of both the context and the nature of ReMSTEP, and the ETMST program of which it formed a part.

Chapter 2

Background and overview of ReMSTEP

Stephen Dinham

The overarching program: Enhancing the training of mathematics and science teachers

In 2013, the national Office for Learning and Teaching (OLT) in Australia called for expressions of interest and subsequent grant applications for a new project, the ETMST program.

The OLT had an overarching brief to promote and support change in Australian higher education institutions to enhance learning and teaching. The OLT attempted to achieve this by:

- awarding grants for research projects
- running awards to recognise excellence in teaching
- supporting collaboration and sharing good practice
- supporting professional development by academic staff.

The ETMST program was unusual for the OLT in that the amount of grant monies on offer was far higher than was usually the case with OLT projects. This was because it was an initiative of the then Chief Scientist for Australia, Professor Ian Chubb. It was described by the OLT as such:

> Enhancing the Training of Mathematics and Science Teachers Program is driving a major improvement in the quality of mathematics and

science teachers by supporting new pre-service programs in which faculties, schools or departments of science, mathematics and education collaborate on course design and delivery, combining content and pedagogy so that mathematics and science are taught as dynamic, forward-looking and collaborative human endeavours.

The program was established in response to recommendations from Professor Ian Chubb, AC, Australia's Chief Scientist, in his 2012 report 'Mathematics, engineering and science in the national interest'. Program funding was $12 million over three calendar years, 2014–2016. Program funding was fully committed to a number of significant projects[48].

The stated priorities of the ETMST program were:

1. Collaboration between faculties, schools or departments of science, mathematics and education, which will produce teachers who have a contemporary and dynamic view of science that can inspire students.

2. Increasing the supply of graduates by, among other strategies:
   - Attracting PSTs from a wider pool, for example, candidates with doctoral qualifications;
   - Increasing retention rates of existing PSTs.

3. Curriculum arrangements that give PSTs of mathematics and science a new vision of how mathematical and scientific content, thinking and pedagogy can work together.

4. Increasing the supply of graduates with an ability to manage this balance.

5. Developing teachers' capabilities to engage middle years students, whether primary or secondary, in relevant and rigorous

---

[48] www.olt.gov.au/maths-and-science-teachers

mathematics and science learning, including inculcating an understanding of how scientific and mathematical knowledge are created.

6. Developing particular capabilities for working effectively with students from diverse backgrounds.

7. Developing commitment to, and particular capabilities for, working in regional, remote and Indigenous communities.

8. With the support of employers, including state education departments, retraining suitably qualified professionals/teachers to expand the pool of teachers with a contemporary view of mathematics, science and pedagogy.

9. Encouraging mathematics, science and education faculties, schools or departments to build long-term relationships with teachers to ensure their knowledge and skills are kept up-to-date[49].

There were a number of stated 'key program principles', chief among these being that projects should involve a number of institutions and that 'All applications must provide for genuine collaboration and dialogue between relevant experts on the interplay between content and pedagogy, as the basis on which authentic learning by PSTs can be built'[50]. This requirement arose from the Chief Scientist's strong and oft-stated belief in the need for greater collaboration between science and education faculties within universities:

> Proposals should demonstrate the applicants' specific capacity to build collaboration, and provide evidence of the success of any existing collaborations, especially between faculties, schools or departments of science, mathematics and education[51].

---

49 Australian Government 2013, pp. 1–2
50 Australian Government 2013, p. 2
51 Australian Government 2013, p. 2

Note: As a result of changes announced in the 2016–17 Budget, the OLT ceased to be funded from the end of June 2016 when its various functions were subsumed into the Commonwealth Department of Education and Training (DET)[52].

The projects comprising the ETMST program

Five projects were subsequently approved and funded under the umbrella of the ETMST program:

1. *Inspiring mathematics and science in teacher education* (The University of Queensland [lead], James Cook University, The University of Newcastle, The University of Sydney, University of Tasmania, University of Wollongong)[53].

2. *It's part of my life: Engaging university and community to enhance mathematics and science education* (Southern Cross University [lead], Central Queensland University, Federation University Australia, University of New England, University of Southern Queensland, University of the Sunshine Coast)[54].

3. *Opening real science: Authentic mathematics and science education for Australia* (Macquarie University [lead], Australian Astronomical Observatory, Australian Catholic University, Charles Sturt University, CSIRO, Edith Cowan University, Las Cumbres Observatory Global Telescope Network, The University of Notre Dame Australia, University of Canberra, University of Western Sydney[55])[56].

Reconceptualising mathematics and science teacher education

---

[52] Australian Government n.d.
[53] www.olt.gov.au/project-inspiring-mathematics-and-science-teacher-education-2013
[54] www.olt.gov.au/project-itaposs-part-my-life-engaging-university-and-community-enhance-science-and-mathematics-educa
[55] Now Western Sydney University
[56] www.olt.gov.au/project-opening-real-science-authentic-mathematics-and-science-education-australia-2013

Background and overview of ReMSTEP

programs (The University of Melbourne [lead], Deakin University, La Trobe University, Monash University, Victorian Department of Education and Early Childhood Development[57])[58].

4. *Step up! Transforming mathematics and science pre-service secondary teacher education in Queensland* (Queensland University of Technology [lead], Australian Catholic University, Griffith University, James Cook University, Queensland Department of Employment, Training and Education, The University of Queensland)[59].

An external evaluation for the ETMST program was also funded:

- *Evaluation* (University of the Sunshine Coast [lead], Phillips KPA)[60].

Total funding for the ETMST program projects listed above was $12 495 000, inclusive of $495 000 for the external evaluation. Funding provided for ReMSTEP was $3 200 000.

Funding for the ETMST projects was intended to extend from late 2013 until the end of 2016 but delays in releasing funding and the project's start (mainly due to the 2013 Federal Election) meant that most projects did not begin until early 2014, concluding in early 2017.

Conclusion

The breadth and diversity of the projects (see descriptions of the five projects in footnotes 54, 56, 58, 59, 60) reflects the complexity of the issues around training mathematics and science teachers and teaching mathematics and science within a broader context and agenda for STEM,

---

57   Now Victorian Department of Education and Training
58   www.olt.gov.au/project-reconceptualising-mathematics-and-science-teacher-education-programs-through-collaborative-p
59   www.olt.gov.au/project-step-transforming-mathematics-and-science-pre-service-secondary-teacher-education-queensland
60   www.olt.gov.au/project-enhancing-training-mathematics-and-science-teachers-evaluation-2013

as outlined in the previous chapter. Consequently, the five project teams formulated a variety of responses to the nine stated priorities of the ETMST program. Because of the complexity of the STEM issue outlined previously, 'quick fix' and/or simplistic strategies are unlikely to be effective in either the short or long term and thus the teams needed to consider varying responses.

It says something of the area and concern over mathematics and science that the five ETMST program projects were so varied in responding to the challenge of improving the PST training of mathematics and science and the support such teachers receive within schools and systems.

However, readers should not construe that ReMSTEP or the ETMST program as a whole has an intent of 'blaming' or 'fixing' teachers. There has been too much criticism of teachers for matters outside their control[61]. It should also be noted that at the time of the ETMST program, there were many other non-profit and for-profit bodies and jurisdictions funding STEM projects across Australia.

Australia needs to develop a coherent and evidence-based strategy to reform STEM teaching and learning in response to twenty-first century needs[62] and it is important to look to the core of experience from within these many projects to develop potentially generative approaches to teacher development.

Discussion now turns to greater detail of ReMSTEP undertaken under the umbrella of the ETMST program.

---

61 Dinham 2016
62 Marginson et al. 2013

Chapter 3

Key innovations and methodology of ReMSTEP

Stephen Dinham, Russell Tytler

Introduction and context to ReMSTEP

As noted in Chapter 1, researchers around the world recognise there are problems with student participation and achievement in mathematics and science and with teaching these subjects. Of particular concern are widespread shortages of suitable secondary mathematics and science teachers, the teaching of mathematics and physical science in primary schools, lower levels of student participation in mathematics and science at senior secondary and tertiary levels, and declining student performance against national and international measures of achievement in these subjects.

A number of interrelated phenomena form a self-perpetuating cycle contributing to this situation. Reflecting the concerns noted in Chapter 1, Dinham has noted[63]:

- Many primary teachers report a lack of competence and confidence in teaching mathematics and science, not having taken the higher levels of these subjects in senior secondary school or in some cases not studying mathematics and/or science at this level at all[64].

- Primary students can develop negative attitudes and mindsets

---

63 Dinham 2015
64 Committee for the Review of Teaching and Teacher Education 2003

about their ability in these subjects. Early experiences of struggle or 'failure', especially in mathematics, can powerfully predict and constrain future engagement and achievement and act as a barrier to learning. Students can see their ability and indeed identity as fixed[65].

- Primary students in Australia perform relatively more poorly on international measures of achievement in mathematics and science than their secondary counterparts, with a general pattern of decline[66].

- There are shortages of suitably trained secondary mathematics and science teachers. The Programme for International Student Assessment (PISA) data has revealed that 'around 30 per cent of 15-year-old Australian students were enrolled in schools whose leaders reported that a lack of qualified mathematics teachers was hindering instruction. The figure for science teachers was around 24 per cent. Conversely, the Organisation for Economic Co-operation and Development (OECD) average for mathematics and science was about 18 per cent for each'[67]. This situation is worse in government schools, low socio-economic status (SES) schools, and regional and remote schools. Some schools 'tick all these boxes'. Some students will not encounter a trained mathematics or science teacher until the latter years of secondary schooling, if at all.

- Participation in the more advanced mathematics subjects and in the physical sciences at senior secondary level is declining. Participation in undergraduate university mathematics and science courses is also declining; with some departments of mathematics shrinking or closing and with physics departments experiencing similar decline[68].

---

65 Dweck 2000
66 Dinham 2014, pp. 8–15
67 Productivity Commission 2012, p. 90
68 Chinnapan et al. 2007

- There are shortages of secondary PSTs in mathematics and science (especially physics and chemistry). Some PST primary candidates struggle with mathematics and science because of their background (some have not studied mathematics or science through to Year 12, or if they have, only at a low level), and they may have negative attitudes towards these subjects[69].

The above represents a powerful negative cycle that must be broken. However, because of the cycle's complex, interrelated and self-reinforcing nature, there are, as has been noted, no quick fixes. Further, this goal is not just about better meeting the needs of industry but of the need for a more scientifically literate and capable population.

Typical responses

Until now, when faced with the above situations, the usual responses have included providing PST candidates and practising teachers with more content knowledge and pedagogical strategies, along with producing units of work and resources intended to make teaching mathematics and science 'easier' for teachers and more interesting for students. Often these resources and strategies emphasise 'hands-on' or 'cook book' practical activities without sufficient scaffolding and background understanding, in the hope that these will lead to greater student engagement. 'Teacher proof' resources can, however, be counterproductive if teachers lack the knowledge or confidence to use these unfamiliar 'black boxes' and either ignore or use them ineffectively. Such approaches also fail to account for the professionalism of teachers, and fail to acknowledge the belief systems that underpin traditional practices that may need to be challenged or renegotiated with teachers if reform is to be achieved. Another approach sometimes used is to provide scholarships to attract additional mathematics and science PSTs. Higher pay (than that of other teachers) for practising mathematics and science teachers has been suggested but teachers

---

69 Committee for the Review of Teaching and Teacher Education 2003

have resisted this approach. And the problem is that none of these measures tackle the crucial issue of why these situations exist in the first place.

The need for reconceptualisation

Additional content knowledge, training and resources can be a useful means to an end, but we need to understand and address the underlying causes of the situation. It is imperative that we take action in primary schooling to influence the mindsets and thinking of both students and teachers. Both groups need to engage with 'real-world' mathematics and science, in the sense that mathematicians and scientists are engaged with solving current environmental, technological and societal problems through particular ways of thinking and working. The thinking behind such problem solving needs to be made visible. In this respect, practice, identity and attitudes are more important than content.

This requires PST candidates to:

- experience mathematics and science through exposure to scientists
- be exposed to mathematical and scientific thinking
- overcome their doubts or fears about their capacity to teach in these areas
- be motivated to engage with and learn more about mathematics and science as it is practised.

Enhanced self-efficacy and intrinsic motivation are key conditions for such improvement.

To this end, education academics and PST candidates need to engage with mathematics and science faculties, and research centres to collaboratively engage in a variety of outreach activities, such as having mathematicians and scientists interact directly with schools. Mathematics and science need to be seen as contemporary and 'alive'—not something archived in a text or online where we already know the answers. We also need to expose undergraduate mathematics and science students to the possibilities of teaching as a rewarding career.

There is also a compelling argument for at least some primary teachers, with suitable background and training, to act as specialist mathematics and science teachers in schools and to work alongside and assist their colleagues[70], something recognised and advocated in the 2014 report from the Teacher Education Ministerial Advisory Group *Action now: Classroom ready teachers*[71].

Primary students in particular need to experience success in thinking about and doing mathematics and science and to see that effort can lead to improvement. They need to develop an attitude that they can enjoy and 'do' mathematics and science, if they are to have any chance of succeeding in mathematics and science in the secondary years and beyond.

To achieve the changes necessary requires both the systemic reconceptualisation of initial primary and secondary teacher education and personal reconceptualisation within the minds of teachers and students concerning mathematics and science.

These challenges, changes and approaches are inherent in ReMSTEP undertaken at The University of Melbourne (UoM), Monash, Deakin and La Trobe universities as part of the national ETMST program.

Changing the thinking of teachers and students of mathematics and science lies at the heart of what ETMST and ReMSTEP are attempting to achieve through exploring multiple models for engaging PST candidates in a variety of contemporary professional practices.

Details of ReMSTEP

ReMSTEP was funded by the (then) OLT in 2013 and was initially entitled Reconceptualising Mathematics and Science Teacher Education

---

70 Dinham 2007
71 www.chiefscientist.gov.au/about/the-chief-scientist

Programs through collaborative partnerships between scientists and educators, and later became known as ReMSTEP. The original intended project outcomes and rationale were stated as follows.

> ReMSTEP will establish a network of four leading universities dedicated to developing new teacher education practices that align contemporary practices in the sciences with innovative and engaging approaches to teaching and learning. The four universities—The University of Melbourne, Monash, La Trobe and Deakin—have:
>
> 1. a variety of teacher education course structures that provide the opportunity to test these approaches in a diverse range of contexts
>
> 2. a history of collaboration between the education and mathematics/science faculties that provide the foundation for this proposal
>
> 3. a track record of collaboration between the education team members on pedagogical research.
>
> The project will support the extension of these collaborations to break new ground in development of:
>
> 1. approaches to teaching and learning that exemplify contemporary scientific and mathematical practices
>
> 2. a framework that will guide these approaches
>
> 3. effective approaches to collaboration between science and education academics that can support this
>
> 4. approaches to dissemination and cooperation that will provide maximum impact in the field.
>
> The outcomes will be:
>
> - Evidence-based development of approaches to mathematics and science education and teacher education that link contemporary practices in the sciences to evidence-based, inquiry-based, problem-solving pedagogies.

- A cohort of graduate primary and secondary teachers better equipped to integrate not just an awareness of contemporary mathematics and science concepts but aspects of actual mathematical and scientific practice into their classroom pedagogy.

- Comprehensively documented innovative pedagogies that are specific to the education and communication of cutting-edge mathematical and scientific practices, implemented across a variety of education contexts and sites.

- Reconceptualised units and mathematics and science educational activities that exemplify scientific practices, together with an evidence-based framework supported by public access resources to support collaborative work between specialist mathematics and science teacher educators and research mathematicians and scientists. It is anticipated that these will be made widely available through a web-mediated environment.

- Innovative and effective teacher education practices that can be articulated and disseminated as 'exemplifications of meaningful collaboration' between the mathematics and science research communities and educators.

- Key principles around which effective dissemination of these approaches can inform the practice of other universities in connecting the sciences and teacher education together with communication principles and practices that can support public understanding of contemporary scientific practices and ideas.

- An established network of science, mathematics and education researchers, supported with an online environment, dedicated to connecting contemporary mathematics and science and associated pedagogies in a variety of educational contexts (including low SES, high non-English-speaking background (NESB), rural, remote, Indigenous).

In terms of dissemination, we intended from the start, and noted in the grant application, that we would make any information, findings or resources arising from ReMSTEP freely available to help the project achieve maximum impact. To this end, we created a website early in the project[72]. Dissemination also occurred through the two annual 'sharing conferences' held in 2015 and 2016 and at annual conferences bringing together the five overall ETMST projects. Various reports to the OLT, the appointed evaluators and this book also formed part of the dissemination strategy.

Nature of the sites and collaborative practices

In the original application for funding, we identified a variety of existing sites where the proposed activities could take place:

- *Specialist mathematics and science centre collaborations* involving staff and students working on modules and approaches for school outreach at facilities such as the Gene Technology Access Centre (GTAC) at the UoM, Bendigo Discovery Centre, the CADET initiative at Deakin (a cutting-edge engineering laboratory hosting school activities), BioLab at the John Monash Science School, and the Charles La Trobe College incorporating Quantum Victoria, a specialist centre of excellence in science established by the DEECD.

- *Teacher education units involving education and science faculty collaboration,* such as science communication project units, which involve students interacting with schools on special projects, project work involving students working with STEM research staff, and capstone units involving students pulling together their mathematics, science and education knowledge.

- *School-based teacher education practices* involving collaborative partnerships between education faculties and schools,

---

72 http://remstep.org.au

including primary science education method units, and secondary placement experiences involving a mathematics or science university–school collaboration.

- *Mentoring/support arrangements involving tertiary sciences students working in schools,* such as the In2science program, which runs in a number of universities including the four partner universities.

- *Visits to research sites,* various university research sites currently host visits and participatory work experience programs for school students. As part of the project, teacher education students undertake extended working visits to the sites, and mathematics and science educators will work closely with research scientists to develop site activities that capture the scientific practices characterising the site.

- Other collaborations involving partners, such as the DEECD's School Centres for Teaching Excellence (SCTE)—The University of Melbourne, Monash, Deakin and La Trobe are partners in one or more of the centres, which promote more school-based PST delivery.

These sites were already engaged in innovative education practices for mathematics and science university students and many of them involved collaboration with science faculty staff. Under ReMSTEP we intend for these practices to be extended to include educational activities exemplifying cutting-edge mathematics and science practices through collaboration between researchers in science and mathematics, teacher educators and educators at these sites. We envisage PST education students and undergraduate mathematics and science students will play a key role in working with such sites to amplify the educational potential of their activities. The sites represented fertile ground on which to develop these new practices with reciprocal benefits for the sites and for translating contemporary mathematical and science practices into school classroom settings.

The innovations

As ReMSTEP was never envisaged as a single project, but rather conceptualised as a series of interrelated complementary activities devised to meet the overarching goals of both ReMSTEP and the ETMST program. Therefore, we decided to group the activities under a series of broad 'innovations'. Some activities were confined to a single university, although activities of the same type occurred at other universities, while others were spread across a number of universities and research centres. Some activities contributed to more than one innovation, although no university addressed all the innovations, at least to a high degree. It should be noted that there were many pre-existing, uncoordinated and unmapped partnerships between university faculties, research centres, teams and individuals and thus one of the early tasks within the ReMSTEP project was mapping these pre-existing relationships, some of which were extended and included under the umbrella of ReMSTEP, although the majority of ReMSTEP activities were new.

There were some changes to the intended innovations as ReMSTEP proceeded from the proposal stage to implementation and ultimately completion, with the following seven innovations being the final versions. As you will see in subsequent chapters, some innovations were larger and more ambitious than others.

1. *Contemporary mathematics and science integrated in PSTs' units of study*
2. *Science students in schools*
3. *Mathematics and science teaching specialisations within primary pre-service teaching programs*
4. *Specialist science and technology centre collaborations*
5. *Exploring models of interaction between scientists and PSTs*
6. *Building on existing student expertise in mathematics and science*

7. *Building a recruitment pipeline of high-potential mathematics and science teachers*

In Part B, we outline the ReMSTEP innovations and some of the activities they comprise.

Integrating cutting-edge practices and pedagogy

To provide further grounding to an understanding of ReMSTEP, the project was based upon the principle of integrating 'real' cutting-edge mathematics and science with initial teacher education, both primary and secondary. The following section is taken from the application for funding submitted to the OLT:

> Every teacher education program must anticipate two communities of learners: pre-service teachers and the students they will teach. In this project, the challenge is to integrate a vision of mathematics and science as dynamic communities of research practice in a way that can be reproduced through classroom activity.

A focus on practice rather than knowledge

A long-standing critique of school science pedagogy is its passive, transmissive nature focused on the resolved conceptual products of science, which misrepresents the excitement and dynamism of the living practice. Joseph Schwab argued that students should be educated in what he called the syntactical as opposed to the substantive structure of the discipline: the way science ideas are posed, experiments are performed, and how data is converted into scientific knowledge[73]. This is echoed in current moves to include epistemic knowledge—about the nature of scientific knowledge building—in curricula, including in the 2015 PISA scientific literacy assessment. It is also consistent with current understandings of science as a discursive practice involving a range of

---

73   Tytler 2007

multimodal literacies that should form the basis of any science education. In mathematics, there is an equivalent advocacy for greater emphasis on problem solving and mathematical modelling. In both cases, traditional mathematics and science teacher education has tended to perpetuate a focus on conceptual products or instrumental processes at the expense of experiences with the way contemporary scientists and mathematicians work in key areas.

From the point of view of contemporary scientists, current science education misrepresents contemporary practice in the field[74]. ReMSTEP thus focused on representing mathematical and scientific cutting-edge practices in pedagogies as part of a reconceptualised initial teacher education to inspire PSTs and, through them, the students they will teach, to see mathematical and scientific practices as ways of working and thinking that can contribute to resolving major contemporary issues. A significant issue with engaging students in mathematics and science is their exposure to people involved in the area with whom students can identify as consonant with their own developing identity, and possible career pathways. We envisaged that ReMSTEP would generate compelling examples of mathematicians' and scientists' work, consistent with this need to generate understandings of the nature of work in the sciences.

Inquiry, problem solving, modelling, context

The focus on cutting-edge science and mathematics practices is consistent with and supported by current advocacy for school mathematics and science inquiry and problem-solving pedagogies, modelling, and the contextual siting of representational work. We intended that the approach taken in linking cutting-edge practice and pedagogy would make particular use of innovative, guided inquiry pedagogy that has been developed and validated over a number of Australian Research Council (ARC) projects[75] and has been shown to lead to quality learning

---

74 Tytler & Symington 2006, pp. 10–15
75 Hubber et al. 2010, pp. 5–28; Tytler et al. 2013

and reasoning, and student engagement[76]. The pedagogy captures the imaginative, often visual processes of knowledge building in mathematics and science. Visualisation and modelling are key literacy competencies in mathematics and science, increasingly supported by digital tools in contemporary practice in the sciences.

Learning mathematics and science is also about connecting ideas to each other. The types of actions students use to build integrated and flexible knowledge networks include connecting, representing, identifying, describing, interpreting, sorting, applying, designing, planning, checking, imagining, explaining, justifying, comparing, contrasting, inferring, deducing and proving. In all of these, the role of language is central. Jay Lemke has said, 'To learn science is to learn to speak science' and mathematical literacy similarly requires proficiency in technical language and in reasoning and argumentation[77]. Promoting such proficiencies requires innovative approaches to introduce PSTs to these new forms of practice.

Another key feature of the ReMSTEP approach was the central role of context. Researchers have often thought of contexts as essential in proving science's relevance to students, or as meaningful conceptual anchors or in developing scientific literacy. Deborah Corrigan and her colleagues have been developing a frame for rethinking the use of contexts in science education. This frame centres not only on the conceptual aspects of science (the individual concepts and big ideas often seen as the products of science) but also on the attributes of contexts, (which are part of the processes and practices of science). Engaging students in different contexts with an emphasis on making sense of such content, using scientific ways of thinking and acting, provides learners of sciences with the opportunities to not only develop their understanding of the products of science, but also the processes and practices that are necessary when engaging with science.

While the focus of the approaches to teaching and learning in ReMSTEP is engagement in quality learning for PSTs and tertiary

---

76   Ainsworth et al. 2011, pp. 1096–97
77   Clarke 2013, pp. 21–33

science and mathematics students, in an important sense these are proxies for pedagogies of engagement for school students, since it is our intention that what is exemplified for PSTs will both involve, and be translatable into, school classroom practices. An important aspect of the project was exploring how to translate sophisticated mathematics and science practices and ideas for different levels of schooling. The project involved working with PSTs and mathematics/science students to explore how best to generate scientific and mathematical practices for classrooms across the primary–secondary–tertiary levels.

Project infrastructure and management

The Acknowledgments section (pp. x–xvii), outlines the ReMSTEP project infrastructure and management, including the chief investigators, the project leader, the project managers (two over the course of the project), the web designer, educational designers (two over the course of the project), project officers, the education evaluator and others involved with the project and its activities, whose contributions are gratefully acknowledged.

Parts B and C

Part B now turns to case studies and examples of activities undertaken under the umbrella of the seven innovations comprising ReMSTEP, which in turn were devised to address the nine priorities of the ETMST program.

The chapters in Part C of this book then consider the overall findings of ReMSTEP and how this body of work, comprising both the ETMST projects and other relevant projects, currently largely uncoordinated, might be brought together, not just for archival purposes, but to make best use of what we have learned and produced.

Part B

ReMSTEP: The innovations

Review

David Hoxley, James Stratford

Introduction

Central to ReMSTEP are seven clusters of university-led education initiatives. These are 'innovations' in the context of science, technology, engineering and mathematics (STEM) teaching both in Australia and internationally.

Universities have a critical role to play in addressing the capability gaps around different parts of mathematics and science education in schools. Each ReMSTEP activity has thus been designed to exploit the special position that universities occupy. Central to this is the universities' responsibility for attracting and training primary and secondary schoolteachers. As hubs of STEM research, universities hold the majority of knowledge capital, and have deep networks within scientific, engineering and education institutions. While the issues around STEM are complex and addressing them requires sustained engagement from government and many parts of the community, it makes sense for universities to focus on addressing these challenges where they can make real and immediate change.

At the heart of this change is a commitment to making a qualitative leap in the quality of teacher training. As a result, there is a genuine sense of questioning and lively debate among education and STEM specialists centred around how to actually fulfil this promise. How do we attract the best graduates into the teaching profession? What motivates them, and, once interested, how can we provide them with an experience of the classroom that leaves them feeling inspired? In the classroom, what kinds of experiences are most likely to succeed in engaging those pupils who might otherwise be discouraged when learning mathematics and science? How do we do this in a way that works for schools with limited resources?

We are asking more of our teachers than ever before. We expect them to be equipped at a higher level: more leadership and accountability; more initiative; higher levels of creativity, resourcefulness and agility. While these attributes are needed across the teaching profession generally, this is especially true of mathematics and science teachers who, over the course of their careers, will rely on high-order metacognitive abilities to constantly adapt and teach in a rapidly changing world.

An implicit theme of the seven innovations (as detailed on pp. 37–42) is that the future of STEM teaching to a large degree relies on the quality of relationships. At the outset, this might sound odd, but as an ETMST program, ReMSTEP has been conceived as an alliance of education, mathematics and science faculties. This can be seen most clearly in those innovations where STEM professionals have provided direct assistance to PSTs in designing and creating teaching and learning resources. While community outreach activities are by no means new to STEM faculty, integrating it into PST training adds significant value to such efforts. It was not only scientists who worked with PSTs; but also, undergraduate and graduate mathematics and science students. Using scientists in combination with PSTs, rather than directly with schools, is one of the key innovations of ReMSTEP. This was driven by the belief that PSTs act as a 'force multiplier', bringing their reflection on practice to the interaction and allowing a richer experience for all involved, including the scientists.

Beyond the university, ReMSTEP acknowledges the important role played by STEM industries, including private research bodies and public institutions such as museums and other cultural organisations. These are often home to great expertise, both in terms of STEM-related knowledge capital, but also in designing and delivering education programs. ReMSTEP has been extremely fortunate to foster and deepen relationships with several key partners including Melbourne Museum,

Deakin's Institute for Frontier Materials (IFM), the Discovery Science and Technology Centre in Bendigo, and Quantum Victoria. These relationships, and others like them, are essential to the future of ReMSTEP, in enriching the training of PSTs and providing an ongoing resource for teachers and their students.

Earlier in the book, we argued that traditional approaches to teaching mathematics and science were of limited success and that Australia needs new ways of teaching those subjects, not just fine-tuning. Through the ReMSTEP activities, guided by the innovations, we can see this reconceptualisation at work with teachers at all stages of their careers, but particularly PSTs. Through guidance from units in their courses, through their own initiative and through institutional relationships, they have engaged with a wider variety of experiences of contemporary STEM practices and ideas, and seen how this can be reflected in more engaging school activities. Cultivating these networks, these relationships that connect educators, students and professionals, will continue to be central to this incremental transformation. The collaborative experience gained by the participants is a taste of the kind of cross-pollination that should be encouraged throughout their careers.

As the following chapters describing the innovations will show, the success or otherwise of a particular activity is also affected by the specific dynamics within and between institutions, and their different and sometimes conflicting motivations. Appreciating these aspects will be critical in understanding why some activities succeed where others are less successful. Even successful innovations face questions of scalability, manageability and sustainability if they are to be part of a system-wide reconceptualisation.

The focus of the ReMSTEP innovations has been squarely set on the time frames of the individual programs rather than managing PSTs' experience beyond the initial intervention. Additionally, the scope of ReMSTEP was explicitly focused on university students (PSTs, mathematics and science students) rather than in-service teachers. A downside of this is that there has been little provision for active support or follow-through. When the new teacher finds work they will need support in the field for the reconceptualisation to become deeply rooted in their personal practice. Looking ahead, supporting early-career teachers by building on the positive experience of ReMSTEP should be a priority. Whether this is in the form of ongoing mentoring or something else is a question that needs to be addressed to capitalise on this initial experience[78]. For educational institutions, this ongoing support also provides an opportunity to build long-term relationships with alumni who may benefit from additional targeted training and professional development throughout their career. And of course, better equipped, this next generation of STEM teachers will also provide a valuable resource for the training of PSTs in the future.

The innovations

Working across a range of activities, ReMSTEP focuses on seven innovations around which activities are organised. These are listed below, along with examples of activities, which are highlighted in the innovation chapters that follow. Please note that space precludes us examining every activity conducted as part of ReMSTEP. What follows is a selection matched to each innovation.

- *Innovation 1—Contemporary mathematics and science integrated into PSTs' education units of study* facilitated collaborations between STEM practitioners and educators to work with both undergraduate science students and PSTs. For example, in two of these activities, scientists and postgraduate research students from IFM worked with PSTs and undergraduate chemistry students to give them first-hand experience of cutting-edge science in an authentic context. Most activities within *Innovation 1* were designed so that the PST would be assisted when designing school teaching resources. The *Engaging in practices of contemporary sciences* activity involved developing and researching a new Master of Teaching

---

[78] Richmond et al. 2017

(MTeach) unit for PSTs in collaboration with Faculties of Education and Science, using reflective pedagogical approaches informed by past evidence-based science education research. The Creation of mathematics teaching videos collaboration between faculties of Education and Science produced videos challenging traditional views of mathematics in secondary schools. These aimed to enable teachers to appreciate the concepts, philosophy and attitudes of mathematics and to provide inspiration for classroom experiences that deal with the ideas (and beauty) of mathematics rather than the technical aspects.

- *Innovation 2—Science students in schools* was designed to respond directly to the shortage of mathematics and science teachers. Researchers have identified this as one of the fundamental contributors to students' poor engagement with STEM at primary and secondary school. At the same time, science graduates are facing increasing difficulty entering the workforce after graduation. *Innovation 2* sought to address these issues by building a deeper level of engagement between university STEM students, primary and secondary school students, and teachers. *Innovation 2* trialled three innovative programs at two of the partner universities, which exposed both undergraduate and postgraduate students to teaching in schools. These included the *School Science Project, Back to School*, and *Science Students in Schools/Science in Schools*. Participating students were provided with multiple opportunities to engage with teaching at different points in their own education. To a significant degree, these activities were enabled greatly by the collaboration between science and education faculties with real benefits for both as well as the schools that hosted these pilot programs. While some activities focused primarily on introducing university STEM students to school experiences, other activities had this as a secondary characteristic. The Communicating Science activity had science and education students planning communication for school students to translate the practices of a research scientist into the school context. *Reconceptualising Rocks*, described in detail in *Innovation 4*, had science students from a university 'science community project' unit working with PSTs to develop communication of geology and museum science for school students. Similarly, Reconceptualising Chemistry paired PST chemistry students with PhD students to plan school activities so that the PhD students got to think about chemistry in schools. This interconnectedness, where activities focused on one innovation while using another as a secondary characteristic, occurs all the way through ReMSTEP.

- *Innovation 3—Mathematics and science teaching specialisations within primary pre-service teaching programs* was designed to respond directly to the capability gap in primary school mathematics and science teaching. Using the base provided by the extended MTeach program, PSTs at two universities were offered new specialised streams designed to deepen the skills base generated from the inclusion of STEM professionals from both within and beyond the university. By working with STEM practitioners in a range of contexts, PSTs were given the opportunity to develop an enhanced understanding of contemporary STEM practice and the communication skills needed to make mathematics and science accessible and engaging using pedagogical best practice. *Innovation 3* is not directly concerned with the recruitment of new teachers; this was the work of *Innovations 6 & 7*. However, by collaborating with institutes and research centres outside the universities, STEM professionals with experience in dealing with contemporary challenges in authentic knowledge creation environments directly contribute to improving mathematics and science teaching. At the same time, through working with PSTs, these participants are introduced into the world of primary and secondary teaching without being directly exposed to the challenges of classroom management. Science and mathematics specialist pathways in the Master of Teaching (Primary) allow students to specialise in teaching mathematics or science from as early as first year. Prior to ReMSTEP, the MTeach program required PSTs to study mathematics and science education subjects but had no specialist pathways. To create these specialisations, existing units were changed to include new electives and designated capstone research subjects in mathematics or science. The Multidisciplinary Science and Technology in Education activity used the strong regional school networks around Bendigo to allow PSTs to design and deliver a unit of study at a primary school in collaboration with scientists from metropolitan Melbourne. This activity addressed another cultural divide, one between young people in the country and metropolitan professionals.

- Universities have traditionally occupied a central position in driving mathematics and science education. However, recognising the crucial role played by other institutions and specialist centres, such as museums, means we can harness their significant and active research and education expertise. *Innovation 4—Specialist science and technology centre collaborations* was designed to leverage the educational value of such sites. While schools have a long history of engaging directly with museums and science centres, these activities refocused this engagement around the development of PSTs and in-service teachers. Like other ReMSTEP programs, subject matter experts and science educators supported PSTs in creating teaching resources. While this enriches teacher training, this experience might also provide a model of ongoing professional development and training. Activities, which focused on this, were primary PSTs at Discovery Science and Technology Centre Bendigo the Gene Technology Access Centre partnership, and *Reconceptualising Rocks*, mentioned earlier, which is analysed in detail later.

- The focus of *Innovation 5—Exploring models of interaction between scientists and PSTs* was to explore purposefully the potential of different models of interaction. Clearly, STEM professionals bring a special depth of knowledge and experience of addressing current issues using the most powerful methods and technologies available, which they have often developed themselves. They can also inspire students and teachers with their own passion, drive and curiosity, especially when empowered with the tools of effective communication; the specialist has a special story to tell. In doing so, the scientist, engineer or mathematician offers much more than knowledge. They may offer an alternative mode of being with which students can identify. Even brief interactions with people who offer a powerful example may have a lasting impact on students' dispositions; more so if the experience is appropriately curated by the teacher, specialist and environment working in harmony. Through a series of activities, *Innovation 5* trialled different modes of interaction with STEM researchers and assessed their potential use in STEM pre-service teaching practice, while also considering the challenges that might occur when embedding these interactions into teacher training. These included: Stem Cell Exploration, where PSTs worked with scientists to produce VCE biology teaching and learning sequences; Multimedia resources for biology and environmental education, where PSTs interviewed scientists to exemplify a biology concept using digiexplanation strategies and animations; and Institute of Frontier Materials research practices video-supported activity modules. A further example of exploiting existing partnerships involves Contemporary Science Workshops, which extended the partnership between ReMSTEP and the AMSPP-funded Advancing Science by Enhancing Learning in the Laboratory (ASELL) for Schools project to generate laboratory learning activities that more directly represent contemporary scientific practices and science as human endeavour.

- *Innovations 6 & 7—Building the pipeline: Recruiting high-potential mathematics and science teachers and leveraging existing student expertise* was designed to increase the supply of STEM teachers with high levels of subject matter expertise. This was done in two ways.

- The first, under *Innovation 6*, focused on increasing the confidence and competence of PSTs by pairing them with subject matter experts who could provide them with a more detailed understanding of contemporary scientific practice.

- The second, under *Innovation 7*, aimed to increase the recruitment of undergraduate students with relevant STEM majors into teacher training programs. To this end, several programs were tasked with raising undergraduates' awareness by offering them exposure to the teaching environment. Science students who are already enrolled in university degrees present an excellent recruitment pool. Still, researchers need to do more to understand why STEM undergraduates are often reluctant to go into teaching. ReMSTEP confronted this directly in our efforts to recruit mathematics and science undergraduates into teaching. Many such students, when shown the professional nature of the teaching experience, recalled negative perceptions and memories of their own school experience. Perhaps they were concerned about losing agency, conceiving the classroom as a place where interest and innovation in their discipline is proscribed. A first-hand experience (especially in the hands of highly skilled and experienced educators) might allow them to create a new and better-informed perspective on the work of the teacher. It is important to challenge the traditional 'pipeline' model and instead envisage a more dynamic identity of mathematics and science teachers, which positions them as STEM professionals alongside other specialist roles.

Several examples of such activities are described in *Innovations 6 & 7*. In the Schools Science Project undergraduate unit, science students developed employability skills through a placement in a school, where they were required to research, develop, manage and teach a science-based module that matched the learning outcomes specified by their supervising teacher. The Monash Science Squad website, run by volunteer undergraduate science students, provides a resource for parents of primary school children to connect with extracurricular activities in science. The *Science Students in Schools/Science in Schools* activity brought together undergraduate, postgraduate science students and PSTs to design and deliver activities in a primary or secondary school. ReMSTEP was able to leverage programs previously funded by the Australian Mathematics & Science Partnership Program (AMSPP) whose charter overlapped with these innovations, namely In2science, the Freely Accessible Remote Laboratories (FARLabs), and ASELL (mentioned earlier). By joining forces with these well-designed programs and adding the dimension of PST and science undergraduate involvement, the resources could be re-proposed and enriched and further supported.

Conclusion

When implementing ReMSTEP, we frequently asked questions about identity formation in participants. How do we enable young people to imagine themselves as the next generation of STEM professionals? How do we do this in a way that engages the desire to learn and explore? We have also asked this question about those who we want to recruit as teachers. How can we help those students, especially the ones who might already be inclined to identify as educators, be teachers? Several ReMSTEP innovations have sought to address these questions directly by exposing school students to STEM professionals and by exposing undergraduate science students to teaching professionals in the school environment. This duality is reflected in the authorship of the chapters that follow, where we see the results of science researchers working and reflecting alongside education researchers towards common goals.

The goal of reconceptualisation is ambitious, and in many ways it is too early to know which innovations succeeded beyond their initial positive intervention. We will not know, for example, which undergraduates decided to opt for a teaching career, or how effective the new teaching resources have been in engaging students in the classroom. In part this is a question of time. But it is also a question of focus, and the focus of most innovations has been on the experience of the PSTs and the professionals they have worked with. Evaluation conducted as part of most activities is very positive, showing that participants' understandings of teaching science/mathematics has been enriched, in particular increasing PSTs' confidence and willingness to engage with science and mathematics topics. Executed with consideration and care, such experiences enrich the quality of the learning experience for school students while raising the competence and confidence of STEM teachers[79].

As seen from earlier examples, many of the innovations overlapped, so that some activities encompassed several innovations. Successful activities were often those that used multiple innovations, all bound by the theme of aligning scientists and contemporary science practice with teachers and contemporary teaching practice. Much of the innovative nature was driven by the collaborative links and structures set up between the STEM professional and education communities. The interconnecting and reinforcing relationships between the aims of the innovations mean that it is possible to harness forces and resources already available in the sector. This is the core of ReMSTEP—all the innovations working together to allow teachers, scientists, students and researchers to reconceptualise the future of mathematics and science education in terms of partnerships between contemporary practice in science and contemporary practice in science education.

The chapters in the next section individually describe the findings from the activities conducted by the ReMSTEP partners, grouped under each innovation. In most cases, there are too many ReMSTEP activities to describe in detail, so one or two exemplars were examined in-depth, and the findings related back to other activities.

---

79 McKinnon & Lamberts 2014; Aalderen-Smeets & Walma van der Molen 2015

Chapter 4

Innovation 1—Contemporary mathematics and science integrated into PSTs' units of study

Deborah Corrigan, Greg Lancaster, Rebecca Cooper, Norman Do, Joanne Burke and Kelly-Anne Twist

Introduction

Contemporary mathematics and science is a phrase that is commonly used, but can be unclear for many. The basic premise of contemporary mathematics and science is that these subjects have evolved and that education about contemporary knowledge, practices and communication in mathematics and science needs to change with such evolution.

Given the dynamic nature of the notion of contemporary mathematics and science, any education in these fields will require collaborations between mathematics and science researchers and practitioners. This collaboration underpinned the portfolio of activities within this innovation. While some existing units required significant modification, we also developed new units to incorporate the contemporary nature of mathematics and science. The activities included were:

- *Communicating Science*—scientists from IFM presented their research to students from education, science and engineering courses. The purpose was to communicate cutting-edge science in an authentic context. Students from each faculty then had to repurpose this communication for their own contexts.

- *Creation of mathematics teaching videos*—we developed and produced three mathematics videos to inspire viewers to think of mathematics as a beautiful, creative and relevant discipline and to provide ideas and activities for classroom use.

- *Engaging in practices of contemporary sciences*—the unit was designed to promote PSTs and in-service teachers' understanding and engagement with practices of contemporary science and mathematics, and how this might influence the teaching and communication of mathematics and science, particularly in school.
- *Inquiry Science*—a topic within the practitioner research (second year) unit in the MTeach course. Students were provided with sample representations of practice to help them link research into their approaches to teaching science.
- *Multidisciplinary Science and Technology in Education* (MSTE)—PSTs worked with scientists to design and implement a unit of work in the field of science and technology at their primary school placement.
- *Reconceptualising Chemistry*—undergraduate chemistry PSTs worked with postgraduate research students from IFM to develop teaching resources to address key criteria such as how scientists develop new knowledge and techniques.
- *Scientists as Partners in Education* (SPiEs)—allowed PSTs to engage with a scientist to create a primary school student activity.

Two of the activities within this innovation will be explored in some depth to provide insights into the impact of these activities. The two activities detailed here are *Engaging in practices of contemporary sciences*, which is inclusive of mathematics, and the *Creation of mathematics teaching videos*.

Engaging in practices of contemporary sciences

The *Engaging in practices of contemporary sciences* activity offers exciting opportunities as it involves developing and researching new PST programs to better address the social relevance of mathematics, science and technology and, importantly sharing these research findings. This activity resulted from collaboration between the Faculties of Education and Science at Monash University. The Monash ReMSTEP team was keen to develop new opportunities for PSTs to experience and better understand many of the contemporary practices of mathematics and science used across industry sectors. The assumption underpinning this initiative is that teachers who are more informed and better able to discuss these ideas with greater confidence and competence in their classroom practice should be able to achieve greater classroom engagement and improved student attitudes and interest towards the study of STEM subjects. The team devised a new MTeach unit (equivalent to 288 hours of study) with a number of key objectives consistent with ReMSTEP. The unit incorporates successful reflective pedagogical approaches informed by evidence-based science education research undertaken by the Faculty of Education.

Key objectives identified for this new unit were to encourage PSTs to:

1. understand how knowledge, processes and communication in sciences[80] shift over time through the influence of social and technological change

2. explore the diverse and changing understandings of the Nature of Sciences (NoS) while challenging participants to reconceptualise and articulate their own personal contemporary view

3. investigate first-hand contemporary practices of sciences and examine how new knowledge created has significantly changed to become more inter-, multi- and trans-disciplinary, for example nanoscience and bioinformatics.

The first objective underpinning the unit focuses on how knowledge in sciences shifts and changes over time and is influenced by technological and social change. Mathematics and science knowledge and

---

80 'Sciences' is used here to signify mathematics and science.

practices are tentative and undergo constant reappraisal and updating. While some ideas prove more enduring than others, all remain open to question. Additionally, the creation of new technology can significantly affect how new knowledge is generated, which in turn can influence subsequent technology development and applications. These ideas, particularly that sciences' knowledge and contemporary practices are tentative and changing, are not widely explored in school mathematics or science classes currently, where content is often conveniently delivered as definitive and enduring. Textbooks are more likely to be revised to accommodate changing government curriculum initiatives rather than contemporary changes in science knowledge, such as new or revised understandings or the impact of technological advances. For example, the recent debate over the changing classification of the planet Pluto or debates about the impact of climate change on structures such as the polar ice caps or the Great Barrier Reef may be seen as revealing an indecisiveness or weakness in sciences' ability to have enduring knowledge and authority. However, such debates provide insights into the dynamic nature of sciences and the need for sciences to constantly reassess and accommodate changing understandings based on the acquisition of new evidence. To ignore such instances of debate and review is to ignore a critical aspect of how sciences are undertaken and that all scientific knowledge remains open to question and revision.

The second and third objectives identify that contemporary practices of mathematics and science, and the new knowledge arising from such practices, has largely now changed to become more inter-, multi- and trans-disciplinary in nature. Emerging areas such as nanoscience, nanotechnology, bioinformatics, and regenerative and imaging technology entail complex understandings of multiple disciplines with research undertaken at the fringes between the traditional subject disciplines. This requires understandings of greater breadth across a number of what were once independent fields of specialisation. Nevertheless, the key processes by which sciences are undertaken and the overarching constraints remain equally applicable. This unit looks to make the processes of sciences and their associated skills more explicit for PSTs and, by extension, to make these explicit to their students as a part of regular classroom practice. The unit identifies mathematics, science and associated technology as a way of knowing and exploring our world, where cross-discipline understandings have the potential for convergent investigation, which can then generate richer understandings and reveal unseen complexity and interdependence.

While some PSTs undertaking the unit may have strong backgrounds in engineering, mathematics or science, including research backgrounds (or even PhDs) in related sciences or engineering fields, many primary PSTs have limited mathematics and science backgrounds. Given this diverse mix of science experiences among the PST cohort, we felt it was essential that all PSTs visit a contemporary research facility where they can meet with and interview practising scientists. The intention of this visit is to provide the PSTs with a 'face-to-face' experience chatting with scientists to explore the nature of their work and the operation and practices of a contemporary research facility. The PSTs then share their reflective insights gained from the visits in follow-up workshop discussions with their peers.

More than 20 expert scientists operating across Monash University and the Melbourne Museum agreed to meet individually with a PST for at least three hours. Scientists approached for this program are engaged in research areas, which help to demonstrate the highly interdisciplinary nature of contemporary research and have a demonstrated track record for actively communicating their understandings of sciences to a wide range of audiences. To assist PSTs to maximise their learning from this experience, we discussed and scaffolded the purpose of the visit in the unit workshops to:

- make the intentions explicit
- assist in constructing relevant interview questions that will explore the scientists' understandings of the NoS
- determine the purpose and range of audiences that they routinely communicate with.

Throughout the unit, we periodically revisit the effective communication of mathematics, science and technology to reinforce to the PSTs the importance of embedding STEM knowledge investigation in a social context. A schema developed by Corrigan[81], attempts to assist the PSTs to analyse the methods and intentions of the different types of science communication engaged in by contemporary scientists. This innovative approach helps PSTs to distinguish between the broad areas of complex cognitive engagement needed for effective communication with different audiences for different purposes. The schema outlined in Table 4.1 identifies five areas of science cognitive engagement that scientists, technologists and researchers are likely to encompass in their work.

Table 4.1: Schema for science cognitive engagement

1	**General public engagement:** This is probably the most basic level of communication, however, even though the sophistication of the science knowledge exchanged is likely to be quite elementary it does not imply that it is not without challenge. Looking to effectively communicate insights into big ideas or complex processes using powerful metaphors or analogies is a creative and often demanding task that confronts many educators daily. Predictably not all scientists are skilled at communicating with the public, which make those that are, such as Tim Flannery, Richard Dawkins and Brian Cox, highly sought after by both the mainstream media and the public.
2	**Informed engagement:** This describes engagement by those who are conversant with a scientific field or discipline. They are informed and seek opportunities to share and improve their knowledge and understanding among competent peers with similar interests or expertise. Amateur interest groups, student societies, professional institutes and associations practise this form of engagement. Examples include amateur astronomical societies, Soil Science Australia, Australian Society for Microbiology, Royal Australian Chemical Institute and the Australian Academy of Science.

81   Corrigan 2015

3	**Applied engagement:** This describes a broad engagement by scientists, engineers, technical designers and science communicators who apply current scientific knowledge to develop real-world applications of technology or provide insights into fundamental processes of science.
	Their interests may include fields such as engineering, medical imaging, robotics, polymer science or nanotechnology. They use the knowledge of science and its processes; for example, experimental design, data analysis and scientific modelling, to test and improve technology and its applications.
4	**Focused engagement:** This includes engagement that deals with the routine practicalities of communication practices within and between scientific or industry research centres.
	Examples could include system approaches for regular reporting on project challenges and achievements to project personal, routine laboratory meetings, initiatives exploring workflow or communication practices and team reviews of technical protocols. It could also include project reporting to industry and government, mentoring practices and career building and management within a specific research field or scientific organisations.
5	**Expert engagement:** This engagement involves science discipline authorities or research leaders acknowledged by their peers as experts and visionaries, such as Nobel Laureates or winners of the Prime Minister's Prize for Science, Eureka Prizes, AIP awards or the AAS award.
	This could include expert analysis or commentaries on new technology or recent scientific research discoveries and their likely societal or cross-discipline impact. Experts regularly provide keynote addresses at conferences and industry, field specialists and the general media regularly seek their insightful presentations and critical analysis.

In addition to using this organisational schema, PSTs were also challenged to communicate their understandings of science using creative multimedia artefacts. This was to encourage them to develop and practise skills in creating and critiquing visual images or multimedia, which has become mainstream within contemporary educational communication. Multimedia channels such as YouTube, Vimeo and Vevo already provide access to a multitude of video resources from which educators can source and share useful multimedia artefacts.

So, an essential skill necessary for PSTs is to select discerningly for quality from these rapidly growing collections.

As a mechanism for monitoring changes in thinking, another innovative approach used in the unit encourages PSTs to review, articulate and defend their personal view of the NoS. While this approach encourages PSTs to develop and refine their views of NoS, it also assists them to form a more coherent view that they felt more confident to share and discuss. Although there has been considerable research into the views of NoS held by a wide cross-section of the community, from the general public to students, scientists and science educators, there is limited research reporting on ways PSTs can effectively evaluate and articulate a coherent personal view of NoS. In initial workshops, the PSTs are introduced to a provocative NoS collaborative card activity outlined by Cobern & Loving[82] where the PSTs are encouraged to work initially as individuals and then form larger groups to select or reject, by consensus, written statements about science that align with one of six broadly identified views of NoS. Through creating opportunities for peer discussion and debate, PSTs are encouraged to construct a coherent personal view of NoS and invited to reflect on changes over time in their positional understanding.

The unit has been adopted because it does not privilege one view of NoS over another and does not encourage all PSTs to adopt one 'currently acceptable' view but instead reveals how contemporary understandings of NoS change and will continue to do so over time. The NoS theme is periodically re-examined at key points throughout the unit and is seen as a mechanism for identifying and tracking changes in individual thinking about attitudes and values of science.

Evaluating the innovation

This unit has been successfully offered twice. All PSTs (n=25) were invited to participate in the research study and completed a preliminary online survey aimed at gathering data on their course pathways

---

[82] Cobern & Loving 1998

and intended areas of teaching specialisation. PSTs were also asked to identify how confident and prepared they felt about the range of skills they possessed and needed to successfully teach science.

At the completion of the unit, all PSTs were invited to undertake a 30-minute individual face-to-face interview with an independent researcher. Eight PSTs agreed to be interviewed to investigate the PSTs' understandings of the course intentions and approaches and to seek feedback on how successfully the PSTs thought that the unit objectives were achieved. A number of the research scientists interviewed by the PSTs were also approached and interviewed, but again only two (n=2) were able to meet briefly with the independent researcher, so feedback about their involvement and interaction with the PSTs was limited. However, all scientists (n=17) expressed their intention to be involved in the program on an ongoing basis and reported that they had enjoyed the involvement.

Results

The data collected from the online survey (n=12) provided brief insights into PSTs' course backgrounds and employment intentions. PSTs indicated that they were choosing to undertake the unit to gain a better understanding of the contemporary practices of science and to develop additional skills and understandings that they thought would be helpful for their professional practice in teaching science and/or mathematics. Not surprisingly, their articulated intentions closely reflected those of the unit objectives.

During a unit workshop review session, the PSTs (n=25) provided feedback on a number of aspects of the unit. The majority of the PSTs reported that creating the multimedia task was highly challenging and generally rewarding. Many PSTs discussed how they did not feel confident about creating and critiquing visual representations compared with the traditional and more widely practised critical essay approach to assessment. This lack of confidence was also reflected in the number and frequency of clarifying questions fielded by the unit lecturers regarding the implementation of this assessment task. This lack of confidence also supports the findings similarly reported by the PSTs that were interviewed (n=8) of feeling apprehensive and ill equipped to undertake this creative task. In general, it was acknowledged that the PSTs lacked confidence in addressing the task of designing and critiquing visual images or multimedia.

One of the surprising findings was the acknowledged impact that the collaborative discussions on NoS had on building the PSTs' confidence and ability to communicate a coherent and more contemporary view of science. Many of the PSTs spoke of how their thinking and view of science had changed during the unit from one in which they originally privileged understandings of science or mathematical content to one with a broader understanding of the processes by which science is undertaken.

> You know you always start this going, oh [I] already know this, [but] ... really talking about it [NoS] and kind of expanding that understanding was really good. ... I came out [after the unit] with a fairly different kind of conception ... than I started with what science is and what's core to it. (PST, *Engaging in practices of contemporary sciences*, 2015)

This shift was evidenced by a number of PSTs in their writing for assessment tasks and during workshop discussions within the unit. There were no opportunities to investigate or witness the implications of this changed view on their professional practice.

On reconceptualising a personal view of NoS, the PSTs reported greater self-confidence in constructing and justifying a personal coherent view of NoS and an improved ability and confidence in discussing and communicating NoS understandings across a range of professional settings:

> I have thought a lot more about the disconnect between secondary science and real science. Without it [EDF5674] I probably would have still taught secondary science in a very traditional high school way. But I am very conscious now of why I shouldn't do that and why I should challenge the textbook sort-of ideas, because it is true that it doesn't reflect what really happens in [science] research. ... It has

given me permission to change the way I teach it. (PST, *Engaging in practices of contemporary sciences*, 2016)

All of the PSTs (n=25) also reported that since visiting a research facility and talking to 'real' scientists they now felt that they had improved understandings of contemporary science practices and how science is undertaken by scientists. Many of the PSTs acknowledged that before their site visits they knew very little of how 'big' science is undertaken in world-leading Centres of Excellence and their views were limited to highly contextualised educational experiences in undergraduate labs or even earlier high school settings:

… it was good for me to see first-hand a lot of what they were doing. The scientist I interviewed, she was fantastic. She bought up herself all of the issues we see with teaching and science and she was emphasising that high school science was too boring and it should be more authentic and it doesn't [at] all reflect her experiences of working in science. (PST, *Engaging in practices of contemporary sciences*, 2016)

Yeah that was really good. I enjoyed … the interview part [of] the site placement and talking to a working scientist and finding out what they value … the importance of creativity and collaboration and what they … know … For example, in science education our experiments work … [this] is not what it's like in actual science. You don't know the outcome of … the actual experiment. (PST, *Engaging in practices of contemporary sciences*, 2015)

Conclusion

The general findings from the interviews, workshops, and assessment tasks suggest that many of the approaches and activities used throughout the unit were largely successful in achieving the intended unit outcomes.

A surprising finding was that encouraging the PSTs to reconceptualise their personal view of the NoS proved much more effective and engaging than originally anticipated. Participants were keen to revisit these ideas throughout the course and to actively explore and debate alternate views. The changing personal view of NoS as articulated by individuals at various times throughout the unit also provided insights into how their views of NoS and contemporary sciences were changing over time. This provided a powerful insight into the impact that robust discussion and debate can have on changing long-held views.

Constructing a coherent contemporary view of NoS also appeared to provide participants with language and confidence to engage in professional discourse, which challenged and further enriched their understandings of sciences. Several participants reported improved confidence and competence in their professional practice when exploring science with their students as a way of knowing and understanding the world.

The research centre site visits and interviews with practising scientists were also reported to be highly informative, and although the conversations and experiences were diverse, the workshop discussions proved very rich in building contemporary views of science practices. From an education faculty perspective, it has been helpful to explore and share the scientists' understandings of the NoS and their assessment of the essential contemporary skills secondary students need to successfully engage in STEM careers. They are quick to acknowledge how rapidly science research is evolving through the development of new technology and advances in information technology and how this poses significant challenges for teachers and science education.

Creation of mathematics teaching videos

Research into mathematics education indicates that mathematics needs to be more than the accumulation of rote facts and algorithms[83]. As stated in the *Shape of the Australian Curriculum: Mathematics*, procedural fluency is a goal of mathematics education as:

---

83   Cobb 2000

> ... mathematics has its own value and beauty and it is intended that students will appreciate the elegance and power of mathematical thinking, [and] experience mathematics as enjoyable ...[84]

However, mathematics is rarely presented in this way, as most mathematics resources currently available are aimed at the mechanics of teaching mathematics or mathematics itself. The collaboration between the Faculties of Education and Science at Monash University aimed to produce resources that challenged traditional views of mathematics in secondary schools. Three videos were produced, aimed at enabling teachers to appreciate the concepts, philosophy and attitudes of mathematics and to provide inspiration for classroom experiences that deal with the ideas (and beauty) of mathematics rather than the technical aspects.

The videos open with the educational purpose and possibilities of each video, while the mathematical content is situated and linked within real-world contexts for the audience to consider. It is hoped that this approach will promote deep thinking and learning in mathematics classrooms[85] while at the same time using the familiarity of social contexts to lead to greater student engagement and improved dispositions to learn mathematics[86].

The three videos focus on parabolas, fractals and knots[87] and while not necessarily directly part of the Australian Curriculum, the intention is to challenge mathematics teachers to be inclusive of contemporary mathematical ideas and consequently broaden their approach to teaching mathematics.

In a similar way to the *Engaging in practices of contemporary sciences* unit detailed earlier, these videos challenge viewers' notions of mathematics. Previewing questions ask viewers to consider:

1. What do you consider to be mathematics?

---

84 National Curriculum Board 2009. CC BY 4.0 licence.
85 Frykholm & Glasson 2005
86 Sullivan 2011
87 Mathematics videos can be found at http://remstep.org.au/

2. Why is it important to teach it?

3. What is the purpose of mathematics in the lives of your students?

4. How might mathematics influence what happens in the real world?

5. How do you justify the inclusion of mathematics in the school curriculum?

6. Can you think of examples of doing mathematics, which don't involve numbers?

The approach taken in the videos is to prompt thinking, engage with mathematical concepts and stop to think some more, while also providing the opportunity for students or teachers to engage in some tasks, such as making a Mobius band with a partner and devising an approach to convince another person that it has only 'one' side and 'one' edge. Each video contains a story of human endeavour in mathematics, which teachers are asked to consider as a useful perspective or not. Additionally, the expertise of the presenter—a mathematician—is also considered from a perspective of influence over the viewer. As a final thought provocation, viewers are asked to complete three sentences as a reflective task:

1. I used to think that a mathematician was … now I think a mathematician is …

2. I used to think a mathematics teacher was … now I think a mathematics teacher is …

3. I used to think a mathematics learner was … now I think a mathematics learner is …

Approach to evaluation

The video on fractals was used with a volunteer group of PSTs (n=18) and in-service teachers (n=5) in a focus group interview process. We taped responses and also collected feedback via sticky notes, which were facilitated by Faculty of Education staff. Preliminary findings from in-service teachers[88] only are indicated below, organised into the three main themes identified from the data with associated recommendations for mathematics PSTs including themes and recommendations.

1. **Interest and beauty are important, but where to next?** Teachers saw the value of using fractals as an interesting hook to engage students but they were not sure how to move beyond initiating interest. The recommendation arising from this theme suggests that mathematics PST education could consider placing greater emphasis on working with and from student interest and provide ideas about how to make links to the curriculum and how to utilise student interest to build lessons and units.

2. **Teachers' confidence and knowledge of contemporary mathematics.** Teachers expressed concern that they did not have sufficient understanding of fractals and were unsure whether students would understand or see their relevance. However, the teachers did not dwell on mathematics content but focused on soft skills suggesting, 'mathematics is important at schools as it develops communication skills, logical thinking, creativity and numeracy'. Teachers were particularly animated about linking mathematics to creativity, problem solving and inquiry. The recommendation arising from this theme is that mathematics PST education could consider placing greater emphasis on working with situations that:

   - make greater use of contemporary mathematics

   - deal with problems that are more realistic

   - provide students with greater opportunity for creativity and exploration. The suggestion could be that more links between mathematics and science could capitalise on such opportunities.

---

[88] PST data is still to be analysed.

3. **Contemporary mathematics versus what's in the curriculum.** Initially, teachers did not see links between the fractal videos and the curriculum and they wanted these made more explicit. However, after watching the whole video, some teachers were able to identify key mathematics areas such as algorithmic thinking, arithmetic, algebra, Cartesian planes, conjecture test-prove, concepts of iteration and coordinate geometry. It appears that the fractals video and the ideas of the 'coastlines paradox' contained within this video seemed to shift the teachers' perceptions of the relevance of fractals and the fourth part of the video provided a concrete example that they could expand upon.

The recommendation for mathematics PSTs' education is that teachers need concrete examples of the use of mathematical ideas such as fractals just as much as students do. These videos are a step towards offering pre- and in-service teachers more concrete examples to support their learning as well as their expertise.

Conclusion

Capturing contemporary practices of mathematics and science for PSTs is fundamentally important if teachers and students are to experience a more authentic representation of mathematics and science in their school education. A number of initiatives from ReMSTEP have addressed this need as detailed here with the *Engaging in practices of contemporary sciences* unit and by creating the *Mathematics videos*. These initiatives provide a starting point for more work to be done in this area, but the beginning of this thinking has been the importance of reconceptualising mathematics and science PST education.

Chapter 5

Innovation 2—Science students in schools

Michelle Livett, David Overton, Rannah Scamporlino, Wee Tiong Seah, Cristina Varsavsky

Introduction

Much has been written about the shortage of quality mathematics and science teachers equipped with the skills and knowledge to engage the interest of primary and secondary students. This, in turn, is proffered as one of the root causes of poor retention of students taking up STEM subjects and was indeed one of the premises on which the ETMST program was funded.

On the other hand, science graduates face difficulties in finding a job in the first months after graduation, with national statistics showing that science graduate employment outcomes are declining and below the national average for all graduates[89]. These outcomes undoubtedly depend on the employment market, but they also depend on the quality of the graduates and what they can offer to industry and employers. A recent report commissioned by the Chief Scientist of Australia calls for universities to re-imagine science education for a future where science is central[90]. The report also highlights the importance of work-integrated learning to develop employability skills that make graduates work ready. Another concurrent Australian study found that science students have very limited access to

---

89 GCA 2015
90 Prinsley & Baranyai 2015

work-integrated learning opportunities suggesting that their university education is largely disconnected from the world of work[91]. To address this, science faculties are making efforts to provide real-work opportunities to science students. ReMSTEP enabled the participating Faculties of Science to include opportunities to science students to interact with school children and teachers within their portfolio of real-work offerings

The focus of *Innovation 2* is to bring together the Faculties of Education and Science to develop new ways of engaging university STEM students with schools to improve the visibility of teaching as a career option for high-calibre STEM students. This collaboration allowed us to tackle both highlighted problems simultaneously. Project partners conceptualised models to help develop pathways that would prepare teachers with a solid mathematics and science background, while providing university STEM students with real-world opportunities to enhance their employability skills and explore career pathways. Furthermore, school students would benefit from engaging with current tertiary science students who bring to schools their experience of contemporary mathematics and science practices and, hence, have the potential to change school students' perceptions about mathematics and science.

There are many examples of involving university STEM students with schoolchildren. Science faculties engage with schools through a variety of outreach activities; this engagement normally consists of activities such as school visits, mentoring programs and events, with university students participating in and contributing to these activities. The In2science program[92], currently funded by the Australian Maths and Science Partnership Program (AMSPP), is a concrete example of a multi-institutional partnership with schools that places university students as peer mentors in high schools that have low socio-economic profiles. ReMSTEP builds on these, and other experiences the participating institutions have, by bringing together university STEM students

---

[91] Edwards et al. 2015
[92] In2science 2017

with primary and secondary school students and teachers to increase the depth and breadth of engagement with school mathematics and science teaching and learning.

A portfolio of approaches

Three different models were designed, implemented and evaluated at two universities. Each institution developed innovative pathways for their students to engage with mathematics and science teaching. In doing so, they expanded the number and breadth of opportunities for their STEM students to engage with authentic workplace experiences. These experiences were chosen to match the flexibility required in a science course, which, in terms of career pathways, is inherently a multipurpose degree program. Students in such courses have diverse aspirations. Some students exit a three-year degree in search of employment, and want to capitalise on real-world experience within their three-year undergraduate degree. Others engage with postgraduate studies, including research and continue their exploration of careers after their first degree. In addition, there are always students who prefer to make the most of their course by combining curricular and co-curricular experiences.

To address the multiple purposes of science degrees and the different ways students take advantage of their flexibility, a portfolio of for-credit and not-for-credit approaches spanning undergraduate and postgraduate science courses was created. The three activities, namely Schools Science Project (SSP), Back to School (B2S), and Science in Schools (SIS) are outlined in the sections below. The responses of students to their experiences were gained from individual student interviews (SSP and B2S) or a focus group (SIS).

Table 5.1 on page 64 illustrates the features of three approaches to engage tertiary students with schools used under ReMSTEP. Each approach is then explored in more detail.

Table 5.1: Three models for engaging tertiary science students with schools

Activity	Undergraduate/ graduate	For credit?	Partnerships	Mechanism of student feedback
Schools Science Project (SSP)	Undergraduate	Yes, within BSc	Primary and secondary schools	Interview
Back to School (B2S)	Undergraduate	No	PSTs Primary and secondary schools	Interview
Science in Schools (SIS)/ Science Students in Schools	Graduate	Yes, within MSc	Science specialist centre staff Primary and secondary schools	Focus group

Schools Science Project

The SSP unit is introduced for Bachelor of Science (BSc) students to provide them with an opportunity to connect with the world of work. This is an elective unit offered for credit that second- or third-year students undertake alongside three science units. The unit was designed collaboratively between the Faculties of Science and Education within the university.

The aim of the unit is for students to further develop employability skills through a placement in a primary or secondary school, which is delivered within the framework of work-integrated learning. Students research, develop, manage and deliver (teach) a science-based module that matches the learning outcomes specified to them by their client (supervising teacher). They work in teams to prepare and deliver the modules, over four consecutive weeks towards the end of the semester, taking approximately 10 hours. The specific learning outcomes of the unit are for students to:

- further develop their general workplace skills, including effective communication with a range of audiences, problem solving, developing new innovative ideas, learning new skills, working effectively in teams, thinking on their feet and coping with the pressures of working in a professional environment where conditions are constantly changing
- interpret the brief from their client (supervising teacher) and research, design and deliver the learning module that specifically meets the brief within the available scope
- appropriately manage client expectations, schedules, resources, risk, personnel (school students) skill and knowledge levels, personal travel to and from site (allocated school), as well as their other commitments
- assess their own understanding of the fundamental science principles relevant to a project and design activities and explanations that will assist lay personnel (their students) to understand and accurately use these principles
- actively seek out and act upon constructive feedback.

Although the core activity is to deliver a science module to schoolchildren, the learning activities and the assessment of the unit are designed to support developing and reflecting on skills required in the workplace. Students are required to participate in a number of workshops in the earlier part of the semester. These are designed to hone their skills in understanding learning theories and link these to effective practice, as well as to provide training in teamwork, effective communication, managing client expectations and reflecting on their own learning.

Assessing the unit consists of several tasks. Students keep a journal throughout the semester to reflect on their journey towards preparing and delivering the science module in schools and the skill set they will require to succeed in this task. After they complete the school activity, students are required to make a group presentation to their peers. The final assessment task is an essay where students self-assess the improvements made in their employability skills and the gaps they will need to address to make them competitive for the future of work.

Back to School

This is a not-for-credit daylong activity where undergraduate mathematics students are paired with PSTs and visit a primary school in the morning and a secondary school in the afternoon. The activity in each school consists of three parts:

1. a briefing made by the school to introduce the vision, profile and programs of the school

2. lesson observation and conducting learning activities with school students

3. informal interaction with school leadership and teaching staff around morning tea or lunch.

The aim of this activity is for undergraduate mathematics students to have exposure to teaching mathematics, to obtain first-hand experience and appreciation that teaching is not just about one's love for mathematics and science, but also about how to communicate that passion to young people. The interaction of undergraduate students with schoolchildren, their teachers and leadership teams, and with teachers in training gives the undergraduate students a glimpse into what mathematics and science education entails from all perspectives and allows them to imagine themselves operating in the school environment. The pairing with PSTs who have prior experience with working in schools is designed to provide undergraduate students with a more structured, informed and less daunting visit. Pairs meet in advance of the school visits to plan activities together. It is expected that this interaction between undergraduate science students and PSTs will extend beyond the *Back to School* activity, particularly during the phase of exploring teaching as a career.

Science in Schools

The *Science in Schools/Science Students in Schools* activity is an elective unit available to Master of Science (MSc) students for credit. It provides an opportunity for the students to immerse themselves in a school environment to gain an understanding of how science is taught in a contemporary Australian school setting, gain first-hand experience and understanding of what is required to be a successful teacher and to develop communication skills with this audience. The Faculties of Science and Education developed the unit in collaboration, and implemented it working with a range of primary and secondary schools. Two of the partner secondary schools have a strong science focus: one collaborates with a specialist science centre, and another is in the process of building a specialist science-based adjunct campus.

The activity involves a school placement of up to 20 hours where the graduate science students take the role of teaching assistants and are guided by a schoolteacher when working with students. Prior to the school experience, the MSc students prepare classroom activities, drawing on the expertise of education academics and science educators from the partner schools or the collaborating specialist science centre.

This unit design allows for a flexible approach, ensuring schools' needs are met as well. Within one partnership school, the graduate science students are prepared in pedagogical and science-based content within the specialist science centre, then work as a team to conduct teaching in low socio-economic primary schools. In another partnership school, the graduate science students engage with the leadership team and classroom teachers to design and develop a program of learning based on the pre-VCE, or VCE curriculum. They work in a backward design model engaging with and teaching progressively younger student teams the science aspects of the project. This model provides a cascading learning effect from upper to lower grade levels, allowing the graduate science students to support senior secondary students teaching scientific concepts to more junior students in the school.

The specific learning outcomes of the unit are for the graduate science students to:

- demonstrate a greater understanding of the conceptual challenges faced when science is taught in schools
- understand the significance of how a science curriculum is taught and developed in contemporary Victorian schools, based on research evidence
- explore issues related to curriculum, teaching approaches and materials related to the learning needs and interests of science learners in schools, as demonstrated through the Tertiary Student Assistant (TSA) experience
- have a greater awareness of the complexity of issues impacting science education, young learners and schools
- appreciate how schools and education systems contribute to society and articulate the range of purposes of communicating about science
- demonstrate improved self-reflection and practical skills
- identify the common features of effective communication in written, oral and other forms of communication.

Outcomes

Each of the three approaches outlined, with their range of student audiences—undergraduate (SSP and B2S) or graduate (SIS), for-credit (SSP and SIS) or co-curricular (B2S), in partnership with PSTs (B2S) or not (SSP and SIS)—provided their own distinctive outcomes. However, common themes also emerged.

The university STEM students identified an increased understanding of the complexity and challenges of the teaching role. They were often impressed by the teaching approaches they observed, the tailoring of learning experiences to the student cohort and the interactions between teacher and students. For many participants, this was their first experience in a school classroom since their own schooling. For participants who attended school interstate or overseas, the experience provided their first insights into the Victorian education system. The nature and extent of students' growth in understanding the role of the teacher, evidenced by the quotes below, indicated that university STEM students may be passive consumers of their own mathematics and science education, and that experiences of this kind can lead to an understanding of the complexity of the teaching role. In interviews, they communicated that the effective mathematics and science education they witnessed was underpinned by relationship-building between student and teacher, significant teacher expertise and commitment to careful lesson planning and preparation, together with an understanding of what is required to facilitate effective student learning and to adapt teacher strategies to the students' needs.

> Normally, teachers are standing up so they are looking down at their students. But the teacher in the class I observed tried to get down to the same level with the students. To me that showed how the teacher could build a closer relationship with students. (Science undergraduate, *Back to School*, 2016)

> I kind of got out of this, was that, the whole kind of commitment that you need to have to be a teacher, like you can't just rock up to a lesson and expect it to go perfectly. There's actually a lot of planning and everything that goes into it, and also kind of building relationships with the students, getting to know their individual learning needs. (Science graduate, *Science in Schools*, 2016)

> Seeing what goes on behind the scenes in terms of lesson planning and organising and all of that kind of stuff was also really interesting, because it's not really something you're exposed to when you're a student at all. (Science graduate, *Science in Schools*, 2016)

> At high school, one of the tasks they have to do is introduce 3D objects to their friends and they have to teach each other about these objects.

So for the 3D objects lesson, the teacher divided instruction into three sections, such as easy level, intermediate level and advanced level. What I learned from this was that they have to plan their lessons around these different categories, so they have these 3D models and the students need to interact with them in specific ways. (Science undergraduate, *Back to School*, 2016)

I think there's a really important balance between teaching and facilitating … if we teach them that investigative style of learning very young they've already got that so we no longer need to be teachers, only facilitators. So that is something we could move towards. (Science undergraduate, *Schools Science Project*, 2016)

I mean generally people say 'oh you're a teacher so you just teach'. But it's not actually the way it is. It's incredibly dynamic and it depends on individuals and your relationship with cohorts and it changes substantially. From class to class, the same cohort even, it's totally different. The same recipe doesn't apply to them all. I realised you need to have that mastery, you need that huge toolbox to say ok, this one doesn't work so I grab another one and try that one, grab another one and try that one. (Science undergraduate, *Back to School*, 2016)

Some of the university STEM students gained insights into their personal interest in teaching as a possible career. In some cases, recognising the intellectual challenge of the teaching role provided a prompt to consider this pathway more seriously. The experience of designing and implementing mathematics and science learning activities also helped students to clarify their intentions. This was an outcome for students in both the longer experience of the for-credit placements of the SSP and SIS or the single day of B2S. The clarification was often triggered by the positive feedback the participants gained from school students who were enthused about learning new science, or learning science in new ways, through the activities.

> It has just made me consider teaching as a career because, despite the fact that I hated lesson plans, actually getting into a classroom and feeling like allowing someone else to understand something that they otherwise wouldn't have and seeing the progress even over just four lessons and then being really involved in not knowing that they could be so involved. That was really inspiring. (Science undergraduate, *Schools Science Project*, 2016)

> I had thought it might be kind of boring like reiterating stuff that you know but you don't take into account the children are variable and that they have different ideas and actually are learning things. (Science undergraduate, *Schools Science Project*, 2016)

The science students were significantly affected by the intrinsic motivation of inspiring young learners to explore science that was new to them.

> I guess I did kind of see when the concepts kind of finally clicked for them, and that was really satisfying to kind of get them to get their head around certain concepts and stuff we were teaching, it was really fun as well. (Science graduate, *Science in Schools*, 2016)

> My main sort of inspiration to possibly being a teacher is just working with the kids and yeah, seeing how they can be inspired. (Science graduate, *Science in Schools*, 2016)

Developing communication skills adaptable to many workplaces was another common outcome, which aligned with the motivation of the Faculties of Science involved. The university students were able to identify student conceptions, begin to develop the skills to design a teaching approach that was fit for purpose and to implement that approach. They also exercised skills in managing the activities of a group of people—the students. These capacities are transferrable into any profession where a targeted strategy requires an initial identification of need and a cycle of implementation, evaluation and strategy refinement.

The project participants recognised that placing young scientists in the classroom also could have an impact on school students' conceptions of scientists and the potential of a science pathway. This recognition was observed in comments of the university STEM students, the school students and their teachers.

> There's sort of I guess an idea for them that science is just not all boring and just like crazy mad scientist with hair in the lab and it's everyday kind of stuff that they can apply … I think even just seeing us being there, they know that there are younger people in the field and if you're just interested in science you can be a scientist, to study. (Science graduate, *Science in Schools*, 2016)

> I personally think, it is a great opportunity for us to learn much more stuff. Because teachers teach us stuff but having an actual scientist come in and teach us and show us, especially because they are older than us, is just a really good advantage for us. For when you grow up. It will be a good step for me when I have to go to college and all that. (Science undergraduate, *Schools Science Project*, 2015)

> It is fun that they teach us. Because we don't have to always be just sitting there at the desk. And being so bored out of our minds. They actually make us do activities. That we can learn. (School student, *Schools Science Project*, 2016)

> They might be a bit young to be thinking ahead five or six years to perhaps what they want to study. But it is broadening their horizon, and it is opening their minds to the thought that perhaps science could be a career in the future. (Teacher, *Schools Science Project*, 2016)

The need for STEM teachers was eye-opening for participating university students, both from the perspective of the shortage of teachers, and the need for teachers who are equipped to inspire school students' interest in science.

One B2S interviewee pointed out the career opportunities they identified:

> When I got into the ReMSTEP program I could see that there are not so many people who want to do teaching in mathematics. So it opened up a new perspective for me. I think teaching plays a very important part in young people's lives. And I think one of the ways that teaching feeds back into the community is education. (Science undergraduate, *Back to School*, 2016)

And an SSP student is now considering the needs they observed:

> I know that Australia is putting a lot of money to getting people into STEM careers to come from overseas. And it makes me sad that like a higher level of science is still not really pushed in schools. There are concepts that I wish … like we learn in late high school, that I certainly think primary age school kid would understand. And I wish that Australia was further ahead, it just makes me sad that it is not. That we don't have such intense, exciting high-quality science all the time. This is just a one-off for them. (Science undergraduate, *Schools Science Project*, 2016)

The opportunities for university STEM students to interact with science-trained teaching staff were also beneficial. In B2S the university mathematics students ran activities in partnership with PSTs. In SIS some of the graduate science students were prepared for their school activities by science specialist centre staff who had entered the teaching profession following higher-degree science study. These partnerships provided informal contexts for discussion when preparing the teaching activities, and when reflecting after the school experience. The times travelling to and from schools often enabled informal conversations about the teaching role and schooling, with the PSTs and science centre staff taking on an interpretive role as the university students reflected on their experience. The university students were able to ask questions about the decision-making pathways these teachers and PSTs had taken, exploring questions such as 'was it difficult to make the transition from research into teaching?' with the following response:

> Actually it was surprisingly easy because the mindset of a researcher is to learn stuff, right, so you're already going in with an open sort of willingness to take on information, you're in that position of learning new things. Alright the things that you're learning are going to be completely outside of what you learnt before, … but if you go in with an open mind about what you're hoping to achieve then you'll get a lot out of it. (Science specialist centre staff member, 2016)

In summary, there were three aspects of the experience that were observed to support the university STEM students seriously considering teaching as a career:

1. increased understanding and respect for the teacher's role
2. increased confidence in their capacity to communicate and contribute to student learning and enjoyment of science
3. the opportunity to probe teaching staff who had followed pathways similar to their own.

Conclusion

Each of these three strategies has demonstrated an impact on the undergraduate and graduate STEM students' perceptions of teaching as a profession, including the complexity of what is required to be an effective science educator and the intellectual demand and potential satisfaction of the teacher role. While the projects shared many common outcomes, the different approaches enabled them to be situated to suit the needs of different STEM student cohorts and the differing contexts within which it is possible to encourage students to take up these opportunities.

The recommendation emerging from this study is to continue to offer a range of programs for tertiary STEM students to engage with schools and their students. These opportunities should be designed to cater for students in different study contexts who can commit to different levels of school experience engagement. The intention would be to enable the participation of students who have capacity and interest to include a for-credit unit of study in their course, and also those who are seeking a not-for-credit experience; to provide short-term and longer-term opportunities, and overall to provide benefit to the greatest number of university students.

Made possible by ReMSTEP, the relationships developed between Faculties of Education and Science and specialist science centres have the potential to endure, particularly with projects that are of benefit to all stakeholders. A feature of the successful partnerships has been to identify a project activity with elements that enable each stakeholder to achieve their distinct objectives. These activities enabled the Faculties of Science involved to provide opportunities for their students to identify and/or develop skills that equipped them for future employment; the Faculties of Education developed a potential pipeline of motivated high-achieving future PSTs; and the specialist science centres and schools were able to capitalise on external expertise in their programs and thereby provide additional benefit to their learners and teachers. Partnerships with schools were pivotal to each program. These partnerships provided benefit to the schools themselves, bringing university students with an understanding of contemporary mathematics and science into classrooms to facilitate science interest and inquiry and to act as examples to the school students of possible outcomes of pursuing further mathematics and science study themselves.

Chapter 6

Innovation 3—
Mathematics and science teaching specialisations within primary pre-service teaching programs

David Hoxley, Melody Anderson, Peter Cox, James Stratford, Nick Tran

Introduction

The most important resource required to meet the demands of teaching mathematics and science in primary education is the teachers themselves. The challenge is one of primary teachers' confidence and competence in mathematics and science. Teachers who lack a deep knowledge of subject matter may consequently lack confidence in presenting mathematics or science topics to students[93].

The situation in primary teaching is different to secondary teaching, where it is obvious that the lack of specialist teachers, particularly in mathematics and physical sciences, is a major challenge. The structure of most primary schools requires teachers to be generalists. The case for specialist training is less clear and needs to be made.

It can be argued that there is a case for mathematics and science specialists to support teachers in modelling practice or with on-the-ground support, curriculum development, equipment management and organising special events[94]. Many primary schools are declaring

---

93 Fennema & Franke 1992
94 Tytler 2010

a STEM commitment, if not specialisation, and assigning specialists to science is increasingly common. These commitments sit alongside long-standing concerns with professional development and support structures.

The Victorian Department of Education and Training (DET) has instituted an innovation in training cohorts of in-service primary teachers to become mathematics and science specialists[95]. The model here is one of enactment and reflection across four domains of teacher learning[96]. This innovation has proven to be successful in raising competence and confidence[97]. However, supporting the creation of in-service specialists creates problems in the school environment around organisation, support and resources. Hence there is a need to train such people through PST education. The federal government through Australian Institute for Teaching and School Leadership (AITSL)[98] recognises this and is also demanding specialisation in primary teacher education. At the moment, such specialists are in short supply. This shortage is felt particularly by schools situated in regional areas, which already struggle to attract suitably qualified graduates.

PSTs have a lack of hands-on opportunities to teach science in schools during their university courses, mainly because, on average, there is limited time spent teaching science in schools[99]. When creating primary specialisations in mathematics and science within primary pre-service teaching programs, we need to consider including a focus on providing mentoring and experiences that build our PSTs' science teaching capacity. This practical application of their university learning, the teaching of science in schools, is an essential component in building this capacity by developing their practical confidence and competence to teach science in schools. These pedagogical approaches stress the importance of exploring subject matter in ways that invite

---

95 http://www.education.vic.gov.au/Documents/about/educationstate/specialist.pdf
96 Clark and Hollingsworth 2002
97 Campbell & Chittleborough 2014
98 https://www.aitsl.edu.au/docs/default-source/general/australian_professional_standard_for_teachers_final.pdf?sfvrsn=399ae83c_2
99 Angus et al. 2004; Campbell & Chittleborough 2014

learners to become aware of and respond to real-world questions and contexts that have direct and sometimes local relevance[100].

The question remains as to what form such specialist training should take. Using the language of the domain model[101], requiring PSTs to obtain more conventional discipline knowledge, may not on its own help increase confidence unless such knowledge moves from the external domain to the personal domain. The essence of *Innovation 3* was to use practical teaching activities, in combination with practising scientists, to engage the domain of practice. In this way, through enactment and reflection, the PST sees the consequences of engaging students through authentic science and enters the workforce with confidence in their ability to engage students with teaching strategies.

In response, several activities were placed around curriculum arrangements, which would give PSTs a new and authentic vision of how mathematical and scientific content, thinking and pedagogy can be woven together. *Innovation 3* was designed to address this capability gap by deepening the level of training provided to PSTs. The shift to masters-level training means that universities have an exciting opportunity to reconfigure teacher training to make the qualitative leap that is required. This can be done by providing specialist pathways and by seeking to evolve pedagogy through cultivating interactions between STEM professionals and PSTs.

This chapter reports on two activities that have trialled specialisations, which address this capacity building using mathematics and science experts as mentors.

The activities

Activities under *Innovation 3* were designed to build specialisations in mathematics and science into primary teaching programs. This was done through the collaboration of mathematics and sciences academic staff and specialist researchers who worked with teacher educators to

---

100   Galbraith 2006b; Galbraith et al. 2006, Howard & Perry 2007
101   Clark & Hollingsworth 2002

develop materials and approaches to content knowledge and pedagogy. Crucially, by involving practising mathematics and science experts, these new specialist streams were created with a strong connection to contemporary practice while aligning closely with AITSL standards. By participating in these specialist programs and pathways, we envisage that early-career teachers will enter schools with a greatly enhanced understanding of mathematics and science professional practice and the confidence, competence and skills needed to deliver according to current pedagogical best practice. These graduates will then be well placed to act as catalysts for improved mathematics and science teaching in their schools. Two activities are described in detail, each responding to the local context: a large program in MTeach at a metropolitan university, and a smaller program in the Bachelor of Primary Education at a regional university campus.

Science and mathematics specialist pathways in Master of Teaching (Primary)

With the support of ReMSTEP, the MTeach (Primary) at The University of Melbourne was modified to allow students to specialise in teaching mathematics or science from as early as first year. Prior to ReMSTEP, the 200-credit-point MTeach program required study of 25 points of mathematics education subjects and 12.5 points of science education but had no specialist pathways. To create these specialisations, existing units were changed to include new electives and designated capstone research subjects, resulting in a minimum of 50 points in mathematics or science. To gain entry into either specialisation, applicants express interest and are selected on the basis of previous relevant study, employment history or other experience in the field. Their results in primary mathematics education, a compulsory first-year subject, were also examined.

Cooperation between the science and education faculties was essential to the development of these specialisations. Cross-faculty collaborations were established through the mathematics and science specialisations as well as partnerships with a range of research institutions, including the Victorian Space Science Education Centre and the Gene Technology Access Centre (GTAC).

In 2016, one-third of graduates from MTeach (Primary) graduated with a mathematics or science specialisation. From 2017, in line with new AITSL standards, all graduates in this program will specialise in one of eight fields. ReMSTEP laid the groundwork to create these specialisations.

The details of the specialisation are listed below. The specialist pathways for mathematics and science are similar. Note that mathematics is in square brackets to show where the mathematics specialisation stream differs from the science specialisation stream.

Graduating with a science [mathematics] specialisation requires completing:

- a clinical assessment in Professional Practice and Semester 2
- completing the elective Science and Technology in Practice (an extension to Primary Mathematics 2 and 3)
- a science [mathematics] focused literature review and project proposal in Researching Education Practice unit
- a science project within Designing Personalised Learning unit
- a science [mathematics] elective in Semester 4
- the science [mathematics] capstone of the Education Research Project unit, to which they are given preferential entry.

In developing these specialist pathways together, mathematics, science and education faculties acknowledged the collaboration as mutually beneficial. Mathematics and science faculties supported the education faculty to augment the content and design of advanced units of study for the specialised subjects. Conversely, interactions with the education faculty, PSTs and school students provided mathematics and science faculties with new pedagogical approaches to teach their respective disciplines.

> I think a great part of it has been working across faculties within the university. To strengthen our programs with the inputs from our mathematics and science faculties, and ... to work cross-collaboratively with other institutions to be able to gain some small view of how things are done in other faculties ... was great. (Dr Melody Anderson, *Science and Mathematics Specialist Pathways* program coordinator, 2015)

It is worth focusing on the science elective in Semester 4, which is a key element in the design of the specialisation. The elective responds to the challenge of determining when, how much and how to best integrate mathematics and science into the learning program.

> You have to talk about [STEM], you have to read about it to make sense of it. For these students, we assume or expect they know what STEM is. So once we have those definitions then we can start talking to them about planning for the teaching of STEM. And that planning, which is the centre for any good lesson, is absolutely critical to know where the learning opportunities are for your students. So you have to plan in great detail ... and it is hard work and time-consuming work for the beginner teacher. (Dr Christine Redman, Chair of the Capstone Experience at the Melbourne Graduate School of Education, 2015)

In order to give PSTs the experience of dealing with this challenge directly, a new elective subject was developed for all PSTs in the mathematics and science specialisations. The subject focuses on an inquiry unit that integrates mathematics and science. PSTs contribute to the design of an integrated unit that meets pupils' learning needs; these units are then trialled in selected primary schools. As with other activities under *Innovations 3 and 5*, PSTs work in collaboration with experts in contemporary mathematics and science to design units that reflect the ways in which mathematics and the sciences are practised in research and industrial contexts. In discussions between PSTs and researchers, there was a strong focus on disciplinary knowledge as well as the identification of and attention to knowledge gaps through formal and informal discussion. Such conversations allow PSTs to identify their own learning gaps at the same time as discovering ways to better use their own personal mix of knowledge and experience in ways that have immediate relevance to their teaching practice.

The experience of both PSTs and school students has been very positive. The new elective subject succeeded in its aim to lift the capability levels of PSTs in mathematics and science teaching while also having a positive impact on the levels of engagement in the classroom. Evidence for this is provided below. There was general agreement among PSTs that, as a result of working with industry professionals, they gained a greater understanding of the ways in which mathematics and the sciences are actually practised while also developing new ideas about how to translate this in a meaningful and engaging way into the school curriculum. Furthermore, through delivering these units to schoolchildren, PSTs gained vital experience with communicating mathematics and science ideas to students while concurrently gaining valuable insights into ways to support learning about mathematics/science professionals' thinking and practices.

The project employed a standardised online survey in 2016 to explore the PSTs' experience with the mathematics or science specialisation. The survey polled 40 PSTs who participated in the activity, regarding overall experience, knowledge change, attitude change, capacity change and students' engagement. In order to explore the long-term impact of the activity on participants, we also gave the survey to 39 graduate teachers who participated in the activity in 2014 and are now in service.

From the PSTs' perspective, all respondents agreed that the overall experience of the activity had been a valuable part of their teacher education. An absolute majority (90 per cent) of responding PSTs felt the activity worked well and they enjoyed the process. Particularly, they agreed that the process has been effective in supporting their learning development. Improvement could be made to provide better opportunities for PSTs to interact with mathematics and science professionals, as three out of ten respondents reported neutrally in this aspect. The graduate teachers shared similar opinions with PSTs in most aspects of their overall experiences with the activity. All of the respondents agreed that the activity worked well and they enjoyed the process. Two-thirds of responding graduate teachers agreed with the effectiveness and value of the activity in supporting their professional development. One exception could be observed in interacting with mathematics and science professionals. Only one-third of graduate teacher respondents, in contrast to 70 per cent of PST respondents, reported positively in this aspect.

The survey showed strong evidence for 'knowledge change'. Nine out of ten PST respondents and two-thirds of graduate teacher respondents stated that they had learnt some useful and interesting science concepts, and one of the PSTs commented that they definitely gained valuable insight into primary science teaching, and valuable practice teaching in the classroom. This activity performed particularly well in terms of showing the PSTs how mathematics and science practices might be represented in the curriculum. All the respondents agreed with this benefit. One respondent highlighted that before the activity they did not realise how easily science learning could be integrated across the curriculum, especially with mathematics and inquiry.

Nine out of ten PST respondents claimed to experience a 'positive change in attitude' towards science and science teaching. The only one who reported neutrally gave the explanation that their attitude had already been positive prior to undertaking the program. This activity has also improved participants' capabilities to provide quality mathematics and science teaching in a number of ways. All respondents claimed that they had engaged in new and interesting approaches to teaching science, such as new models, new questioning techniques and new resources. The two groups of respondents also highlighted the benefits of learning ways of engaging with contemporary science that will influence their teaching in the future and of gaining experience in understanding and communicating mathematics and science ideas to students.

The two groups of respondents had slightly different opinions of their benefits in gaining ideas on bringing contemporary science practices into the school curriculum. All responding PSTs reported positively on this aspect, while two-thirds of graduate teachers reported in the same way. In addition, 90 per cent of PST respondents and two-thirds of graduate teacher respondents reported that they gained valuable ideas about how to support students to learn about what mathematics and science professionals do and the way they think. For example, a PST respondent described learning engineering IDPE (investigate, design, produce, evaluate) design processes and ways to incorporate problem solving, creativity, curiosity and critical thinking. As a result of the activity, all responding participants grew their confidence in teaching the relevant subject in school.

According to the respondents' feedback, their students benefitted through the activity in different ways, including developing new understanding of the nature of scientific practices, and productive engagement with learning science. According to the two group responses, as a result of the activity, students were 'more likely to be engaging with science learning', particularly those learning activities infused with contemporary scientific practices. However, a considerable number of respondents were neutral about the new understanding of the nature of scientific practices that students could develop. This is an area where further work is needed.

Overall, the way that the activity combined the elements of authentic science practice, science discipline knowledge and hands-on implementation has shown to be a powerful way of changing PST perceptions of their own efficacy in teaching science at primary school. What remains to be seen is how this change translates to the school environment when they enter the workforce.

Multidisciplinary Science and Technology Integrated Experience

The Multidisciplinary Science and Technology Integrated Experience (MSTIE) unit at La Trobe University was designed to increase primary PSTs' confidence and competence in teaching science. This was achieved by enabling the PSTs to teach an entire integrated science unit in a primary school. They used problem-based learning to link a unit in the third year of their Bachelor of Science (Primary) with both a three-week professional experience (placement) unit and a design and technology unit. The problem that was assessed across all three units was:

> To address the need for more graduates from STEM courses we need to engage primary school students in STEM. In teams of two you are to cooperatively design, plan, teach and evaluate an integrated STEM unit as a part of your professional experience.[102]

Tasked with creating this integrated STEM unit for their placement, students received advice from expert academic staff from the School of Molecular Sciences at La Trobe University. These scientists met with and advised students on strategies PSTs could employ to deliver their lessons in an interactive and engaging way. Students were also provided with materials and equipment from the School of Molecular Sciences, such as solar-powered cars that students could build in class and other consumables, which would not have ordinarily been available to the PSTs on their school placements. The scientists also linked students with appropriate scientists who could lead engaging incursions involving activities and materials that are not normally available within primary schools.

Overall, the experience was positive for both the PSTs and the primary school students involved. Over the three years, there were 45 third-year PSTs involved (2014 = 10, 2015 = 14, 2016 = 21). The model evolved over the three years. Initially, science discipline experts were linked with PSTs to support existing MSTIE practices. In later years, generic scientists worked alongside PSTs to develop the activities to be delivered to schools. It was found that scientists who were not experts in the particular topic often found it easier to work with PSTs to craft engaging activities at an appropriate level.

The pilot year in 2014 found that the use of a science discipline expert was problematic, as the scientists were chosen for their discipline expertise and not their ability to communicate with primary school

---

102   MSTIE unit Student Learning Guide, 2015. Copyright Latrobe University.

students. As a result, while the PSTs found the scientists extremely knowledgeable and able to help them understand the science concepts they were teaching, in all but one case the scientist was not willing to work with, or not suitably skilled to communicate with, primary school students in an excursion or incursion. This limited the success of the pilot year. In subsequent years the activity was change so PSTs could work with generic scientists who were better communicators and enthusiastic about working with the PSTs and their primary school students. This approach was a much more productive arrangement of scientists with PSTs in the MSTIE unit.

The 14 participants in 2015 were asked to complete a survey following their experience, which garnered a 50 per cent response rate. The Likert scale responses were coded from 1 (strongly disagree) to 5 (strongly agree) and the average PST responses are summarised in Table 6.1.

Table 6.1: Average Likert responses to survey questions with indicative quotes

Question	Response
As a result of ReMSTEP, do you feel you are more confident teaching science in the classroom?	4.6
As a result of ReMSTEP, would you approach a scientist when developing lesson plans in future?	4.9
The scientist I worked with was very helpful.	4.7
The scientists' specific knowledge about their discipline helped to plan my lessons.	4.3
The scientist provided me with ideas for equipment and activities.	4.6
The scientist was willing to visit my school.	4.9
I enjoyed the overall ReMSTEP experience.	4.6

From Table 6.1, we can see that the students reported very positively on their experience. Additionally, self-reported responses indicated that all PSTs felt more confident about teaching science after the experience, were willing to approach scientists when developing science lessons, and enjoyed the interaction with the scientists. In this year, all scientists ran an excursion or incursion with their PST's primary school students. After the unsuccessful pilot year, it was a relief to see the high rating on the helpfulness of the scientists, their specific discipline knowledge and ideas for equipment and activities. Compared to 2014, the most pleasing outcome was the reporting of their willingness to do school visits or excursions (or both in two cases). The success of the 2015 iteration was to select generic scientists with a willingness and ability to cooperatively work with non-scientist PSTs to enrich a primary school science and technology unit.

The responses to the open-ended question 'Did ReMSTEP allow you to achieve anything that you otherwise couldn't have done? Explain.' were extremely positive. All seven PSTs reported that the interaction with ReMSTEP and the scientist did help to achieve things that couldn't otherwise occur. The three main themes in the PST responses to this question were access to: equipment (5 responses), resources (3 responses), and an expert incursion visitor (5 responses).

A related open-ended question asked 'Did your interaction with your scientist enhance what you did with your placement and the topics you were teaching?' The responses to this question were equally positive and a brief comment highlights the authenticity that the interaction with the scientist created in designing and teaching the science unit:

> Yes, it made the experiences richer, engaging and more authentic. (PST, MSTIE, 2015)

Many PSTs recognised the benefits of ReMSTEP to the broader picture of their future science teaching:

> During the planning stages of MSTIE we were given the opportunity of getting in contact with a working scientist from ReMSTEP. We had a fantastic experience with this organisation, as we were able to use their expertise to help us provide students with rich and engaging experiences. Making the effort to get involved with these types of programs, or with local universities or expert community members enables teachers to expose students to complex concepts in

an authentic and meaningful way. Scientists from this program were able to provide us with the resources and knowledge to create beautiful borax crystals, the success of this experiment helped develop our confidence in conducting further experiments with the students. We highly encourage teachers to reach out further than just textbooks and truly engage with the wider community to provide better outcomes for students. (PST, MSTIE, 2015)

Working with scientists to create engaging incursions was not only beneficial for the PSTs, but also for the teachers and children in the schools (as shown in Figure 6.1).

For children to see a real live scientist in operation has been a wonderful experience for them and it has further expanded and consolidated their understanding of the topic we are studying. (Schoolteacher, MSTIE, 2015)

Figure 6.1: Year 1 Girton Grammar student exploring the borax crystals they grew under the direction of a synchrotron scientist[103]

103   Source: ReMSTEP 2018

Conclusion

In creating primary specialisations, we need to consider the practical application of the PSTs' learning. Both these trials involved the design and teaching of mathematics and science units in schools and this opportunity to trial their ideas in the primary classroom benefits PSTs' confidence and competence when teaching these subjects. This could be a key finding—that primary teaching courses should consider providing the opportunity for PSTs to teach science and that these two activities provide ways in which this can be achieved within existing university structures. A further benefit is that schools where these PSTs are placed are getting well-resourced, high-quality science teaching; something that research has shown is not currently occurring in all schools.

There are clear benefits to PSTs working with scientists to enrich the classroom teaching experience. This is possible through the scientists' ability to mentor PSTs to aid in their understanding of science concepts, to provide appropriate activity ideas and expertise for using materials such as liquid nitrogen, to supply equipment and resources, and to assist with incursions or excursions.

Additionally, providing well-resourced PSTs to teach in schools provides professional development and modelling to established schoolteachers. Like the science specialists introduced into Victorian schools, these PSTs can provide gentle mentoring and have the potential to increase classroom teachers' capacity to teach science. Key to this effectiveness is the representation of contemporary science practice by both teachers and students, leading to a rich and authentic engagement.

Chapter 7

Innovation 4—Specialist science and technology centre collaborations

Leissa Kelly, Maria Gibson

Introduction

An important part of ReMSTEP was to create critical links and connections to facilitate best practice for teaching and learning. This was achieved in *Innovation 4* by working with specialist science centres to link PSTs with scientists.

These collaborations enabled the PSTs to engage with contemporary science, the practice of scientists and the process of science. They also enabled high-calibre science students to engage with primary and/or secondary school students and allowed them to work collaboratively with PSTs, centre staff and scientists to develop high-quality resources to use in schools.

Successful partnerships between universities offering teacher education programs and specialist science centres are collaborative in nature and are based on 'trust, mutuality and reciprocity'[104]. There are many advocates for these types of collaborative partnerships[105] mainly because they enable teacher education within authentic learning environments that promote cooperative learning. According to Lederman[106], PSTs need to actually '*see* science at work' in order to internalise the science and fully understand the extent to which it is

---

104 Kruger et al. 2009
105 Chesebrough 1994; Paris 1997; Jung & Tonso 2006
106 Lederman 1999

an intrinsic part of our everyday lives.

ReMSTEP partnerships were established with three specialist science and technology centres around Victoria:

- Gene Technology Access Centre (GTAC), Parkville
- Discovery Science and Technology Centre, Bendigo
- Melbourne Museum, Carlton

These partnerships are described below.

Gene Technology Access Centre

PSTs and academics from two universities worked with scientists and GTAC staff to develop school units that incorporated cutting-edge science research. These units were based on contemporary research about the bionic eye (Years 8–9), stem cell therapy (Year 8 and VCE), and adaptations (Years 5–6).

Initial workshops aimed at planning and designing units of work based on contemporary science issues were held at GTAC in Parkville. During these workshops, volunteer PSTs enrolled in teacher education programs at Melbourne and Deakin Universities met with research scientists, educational staff from GTAC, and science and education academic staff from both universities.

Discovery Science and Technology Centre

The *Discovery Science and Technology Centre Bendigo* (Discovery Centre) activity involved 160 undergraduate PSTs collaborating with Discovery Centre experts to plan and run a science excursion for all classes in four local low socio-economic schools. This large undertaking involved 50 classes of primary school children. The PSTs were directed to write a unit plan for a real class that involved an excursion to the Discovery Centre during the 'explore' phase of the Primary Connections 5Es model[107].

---

107 Primary Connections 5Es model: engage, explore, explain, elaborate and evaluate

There was an expectation that each PST would get to know their class by leading the teaching of an 'engage' activity prior to running the excursion. The goal was to provide the PSTs with practical experiences of teaching science using the Primary Connections 5Es model, and using the Primary Connections' units as the initial base for their activity that they then modified for their class, in consultation with their supervising teacher. After the visit to the Discovery Centre, the PSTs developed a design- and technology-based lesson to use in the 'elaborate' or 'evaluate' phase of the modified Primary Connections 5Es unit.

The Discovery Centre activity has been very successful. It is a sustainable model where PST teams liaise with Discovery Centre experts to tailor an excursion for their class based on prior knowledge uncovered during the 'engage' phase of the unit. The benefits for the PSTs are that they see a Primary Connections 5Es unit in action, they engage with a classroom teacher in its delivery and they work with science experts at the Discovery Centre to deliver a tailored program for their class. The schoolteachers benefit from a tailored Primary Connections 5Es unit and the primary students are treated to an engaging and well-resourced science unit involving an excursion. Post-ReMSTEP, the activity has continued with funding from local philanthropic sources.

Melbourne Museum

Collaboration between two universities and Melbourne Museum saw the development of an activity titled *Reconceptualising Rocks*. This activity enabled PSTs to work with research geologists from Melbourne Museum to develop their scientific thinking through authentic learning experiences and to connect to contemporary science and museum pedagogical practices. Students were shown how to recognise and interpret field evidence to explain the geologic past and predict the geologic future. Students also worked in teams to produce curriculum materials to support teaching earth science.

Each of the three partnerships described involved significant participation by PSTs and by the practising scientists, and many of the findings arising from these activities and partnerships are similar.

As mentioned, the Melbourne Museum partnership involved two universities and a specialist science centre, and thus it is used as an exemplar for the remainder of this chapter.

Undergraduate science students participated alongside PSTs enrolled in both undergraduate and master's courses. In the description that follows, the word 'student' is used to describe this mixed cohort.

Reconceptualising Rocks

Organisations such as Melbourne Museum provide many educative opportunities and resources for both pre-service and graduate teachers. These include highly developed educational programs, extensive exhibits and archival materials, current research data and links to research scientists.

Through the partnership between ReMSTEP and Melbourne Museum, PSTs were connected with contemporary museum practices in learning and teaching science. The focus of the initiative was to:

- improve the competence and confidence of participating PSTs when teaching and learning earth sciences
- increase PSTs' understandings of science processes
- provide the PSTs with insight into the role of the scientist
- provide a model for PSTs to translate science ideas and practices for educational purposes.

This was done through exploring pedagogical approaches to teaching earth sciences, rather than delivering content knowledge. Melbourne Museum education staff and scientists delivered the activity, with Melbourne Museum acting as a contextual setting. This provided PSTs with expertise from an organisation that is a key communicator of science in Victoria and that is a contemporary site for learning.

The project was designed around three separate elements that were closely embedded in the structure of the program:

1. an *immersion* experience that provided the students with an *authentic* experiential learning opportunity

2. enrichment of the participants' conceptual science understandings by connecting them to *contemporary museum and scientific practices*

3. enabling the students to explore *innovative pedagogical approaches and practices*[108].

Throughout the *Reconceptualising Rocks* activity, students were encouraged to view geology as a forensic science, underpinned by the fundamentals of chemistry, physics, mathematics and biology. By taking part in the activity, they gained insight into the importance of geological sciences and the understanding that it is a dynamic science where new discoveries are being made.

The activity

The activity was delivered in three parts, primarily based at the Melbourne Museum. On Day 1, students had the opportunity to explore the museum's geological specimens in the Dynamic Earth gallery before being taken on a guided tour of the gallery by the museum's lead geologist. By creating mind-maps, the students were able to scaffold the new insights they had gained, before taking part in a Rocks–Camera–Action education program, experienced as a Year 8 student. This culminated in the students, armed with GoPro portable video cameras and iPads, making short films about the gallery collection that reflected their prior knowledge, their new learnings and how their understanding of earth science had changed over the course of the day.

For the second part of the activity (Day 2), the students were taken on a back-of-house tour to talk to the scientists about their current research and work practices, and to see a small part of the extensive minerals and rock collection held at the museum (Figure 7.1).

---

108 Dawborn-Gundlach et al. 2017

Innovation 4

Figure 7.1: a. Melbourne Museum research scientist showing students samples collected on recent fieldtrips; b. Melbourne Museum research scientist, Dr David Pickering, discusses a recent discovery of dinosaur bones and the impact this had on understanding the species' physiology.[1]

1   Source: Elke Barczak, Museum Victoria

This proved to be a valuable and enlightening experience for the students, enabling them to gain insight into how and why the Melbourne Museum specimens and collections were used to create new knowledge. At the same time, this introduced the students to the importance of earth science to the community – to help solve important environmental issues – and to contemporary approaches to research.

Day 3 (the third part of the activity) comprised a full-day field trip to geologically rich sites in Victoria: Phillip Island; the Organ Pipes National Park in Keilor; or Hanging Rock State Park (Mount Diogenes) in the Macedon Ranges. These important natural microcosms of Victorian geology provided examples of some of the oldest Victorian rock formations ranging from the Cambrian period (540–490 million years ago) through to the youngest Quaternary rocks (from about 11 000 years ago). The geological richness of these sites allowed the students to explore directly metamorphic, igneous and sedimentary rock types *in situ*. Importantly, visiting these sites enabled the Melbourne Museum geologist to demonstrate how to 'read the rocks of the landscape' and to show the students that the 'present is the key to the past', thereby bringing geology 'alive'[109].

Throughout all parts of the *Reconceptualising Rocks* activity, students were encouraged to:

- collect specimens while in the field

- photograph field sites, or exhibitions or specimens in the collection

- learn about the geology of the area

- to work in groups, using the GoPros and iPads, to create a digital resource for future use in their classroom.

---

[109] Melbourne Museum geologist, Reconceptualising Rocks, 2016

Figure 7.2: Reconceptualising Rocks, Phillip Island field trip[110]

Impacts of the activity

The pedagogical approach of integrating PST education with the learning space, contemporary teaching practices, and expertise of scientists from the museum, proved a highly successful developmental forum for the students. Impacts of the *Reconceptualising Rocks* activity on PSTs included improved understanding of:

- the role of the museum as an educational resource
- the role of the museum in supporting contemporary earth science and its relevance to education
- the practice of museum scientists and their role with the museum as educators, active researchers and collaborators with other researchers and industry
- science and science teaching and learning.

---

110 Source: Elke Barczak, Museum Victoria

Students also improved their capability and confidence to teach science (particularly geoscience). An added benefit was that each student left the activity with the digital resource and/or lesson plans that they had developed with their team members and that they could use in their future teaching careers. More importantly, perhaps, the students acquired the skills and direct experience necessary to create new resources in the future. One student commented that:

> … [the program] gave me an insight as to how to incorporate different activities into a lesson plan than just theoretical methods of learning. (PST, *Reconceptualising Rocks*, 2016)

Similarly, another student noted that:

> … the use of a concept map helped, and I can see myself doing that with my students. Incorporating media/video presentations is something I would definitely like to do. (PST, *Reconceptualising Rocks*, 2015)

Exposure to the museum as a site of teaching and learning facilitated a shift in PST perceptions. Although most PSTs recognised the museum as a venue that could be used by teachers to assist student learning, many did not realise the depth of the role played by the museum in information and resource sharing, nor its function as a research centre in its own right.

The students were surprised at the amount and quality of work required to develop and produce the museum's high-calibre learning experiences. The essential role of the scientists in designing exhibits and educative programs, and in preparing educative staff to deliver the programs occurs behind the scenes. When students could talk to Melbourne Museum scientists, they gained insight into the depth of research and cutting-edge science that went into designing and developing the Museum's collections, galleries and education programs. This was evidenced by the following students' comments:

> I particularly felt that the first day in the museum really enhanced my understanding of earth science and highlighted the vital role of the museum in sharing this information. (PST, *Reconceptualising Rocks*, 2015)

> The amount of work scientists put in is a lot more than I had initially anticipated. (Science student, *Reconceptualising Rocks*, 2016)

Reconceptualising Rocks also was highly successful in facilitating an attitudinal change in participating students—85 per cent of PSTs left feeling very positive about the inclusion of earth sciences within the secondary science curriculum. Of 26 responses to a question in the 2015 survey concerning this topic, 85 per cent (22 responses) were positive. The remaining 15 per cent came into the program already aware of its importance, which was confirmed by participation in the program.

Students also came away with an expanded perception of the nature and relevance of earth science, including a better understanding of what it is about, how it relates to other subjects within the curriculum, its dynamic nature and how it relates to the world around us and life in general. Prior to the *Reconceptualising Rocks* activity, few students realised that the museum played a role in supporting contemporary earth science. One student shared the following:

> I have noticed a change in that I now see that geology is an evolving science that has a role in the future of our earth and is not just a science of learning about the past. I can now see the importance of this science in our everyday lives and think it is important that students are made aware of this. (PST, *Reconceptualising Rocks*, 2015)

Another student's comment reflected the general lack of understanding of museums as research centres:

> I wasn't aware that research scientists worked in museums. (Science Student, *Reconceptualising Rocks*, 2015)

Overall, participants gained a good understanding of the work of scientists and their research, development practices and roles. Student comments reflected these insights particularly in relation to the scientists' role in education, research and liaison with industry and other researchers:

> I didn't realise that they (research scientists) were in charge of both research in the labs as well as running the exhibitions. (PST, *Reconceptualising Rocks*, 2015)

> I learnt that they (research scientists) are still researching every day and always work in collaboration with many organisations. (Science student, *Reconceptualising Rocks*, 2015)

The focus groups highlighted the importance of contact with research scientists in teacher education. In particular, students commented on the level of knowledge of the head geologist participating in the activity and his passion for his work sparked PST interest for geology (Figure 7.3). His ability to read the landscape on field trips brought the topic alive and, in doing so, he was able to demonstrate that rocks *in situ* can say more about a place than 'rocks in a box'. This had a profound impact on the group. This experience was frequently compared to the perceived boring manner in which they had been taught earth science at school. These unpleasant recollections of learning a science subject have now been replaced by new positive perceptions of the same subject:

> I found earth science not as interesting as other science areas during my secondary school experience. However, this program allowed me to understand how interesting earth science can be when presented by passionate and knowledgeable individuals. (PST, *Reconceptualising Rocks*, 2015)

Such comments highlight what can be achieved by leveraging the combination of subject matter experts and the natural environment to provide an inspiring and effective learning experience. They also

Innovation 4 101

Figure 7.3: a. A geologist pointing out rock formations in roadside cuttings; b. Students exploring 'The Giant's Steps' at Organ Pipes National Park with a geologist.[111]

reflected the strong educational role that research scientists can play in teacher education programs. One student commented:

> The field trip was fantastic in revealing the presence of important geological examples in the local environment. It was great to see how this concept could be translated into any geological sites around the area local to a secondary school. (PST, *Reconceptualising Rocks*, 2016)

The success of a program such as this relies heavily on the degree to which students leave feeling more confident and capable as teachers themselves. On this point, PSTs noted:

> I feel the time in the museum is the part of the program that is most transferable to the classroom. While the field trip was a wonderful

---

111   Source: Elke Barczak, Museum Victoria

experience and would be a great learning experience for students the practicality of delivering this as a part of the curriculum may not always be possible. (PST, *Reconceptualising Rocks*, 2015)

I have gained confidence when presenting as I have more knowledge in geology and teaching. Still need more but I have come a long way. (PST, *Reconceptualising Rocks*, 2016)

Such comments highlight not merely the value of the museum as an effective training context for PSTs, but the benefit of working with science organisations where teaching is at the core of their day-to-day operations. The Melbourne Museum is staffed with a blend of subject-matter experts and skilled education professionals, many of whom have worked in primary and secondary school environments quite apart from running educational programs within the museum.

The activity also benefited the scientists working at Melbourne Museum. It helped to improve their skills in science communication and teaching; exposed them to new pedagogical approaches; provided insights into how the museum and the work of museum scientists are perceived by PSTs, and how the field of earth sciences, specifically geology, is perceived (very few of the PSTs had undertaken any earth science units in their undergraduate courses). Moreover, the activity helped the scientists to develop a better understanding of how university students learn and the current teaching process. This is valuable as there are few opportunities for most scientists working in science centres to be directly involved in classroom teaching activities.

The principal Melbourne Museum scientist involved in the *Reconceptualising Rocks* activity commented that his participation made him more aware of how he presented material, and that scientists did not always have the ability to translate their research into a language easily understood by those from other walks of life:

… it does make me actually have to become a bit more self-aware about how I present things. The scientists don't always have that ability to translate their own research into the everyday language for people from all walks of life and make it understandable. (Scientist, *Reconceptualising Rocks*, 2015)

These findings and responses were echoed in the other two activities described earlier in this chapter.

The longer-term implications for this activity, as suggested by the evidence, are informed teachers able to share their experiences with future colleagues and who will continue to develop ongoing relationships with scientists in a way that will support continual learning over years to come. By doing so, teachers will refresh and build their understanding of contemporary science in ways that can be incorporated into their classrooms. The positive experiences of PSTs in the *Reconceptualising Rocks* activity also benefit Melbourne Museum, as the PSTs would become excellent ambassadors of the museum. Once they have become teachers they would be inclined to suggest students visit the museum and continue the collaboration.

Collaboration and networks/partnerships: Making them work

The success of the collaborative activity is underpinned initially by the open discussions during the planning stages of the activity. This was seen clearly in the discussions with the Melbourne Museum where a clear strategic direction emerged from the start. Each stakeholder group had its own educative objectives to meet and these always needed to be considered in the planning phase. In ensuring these needs were met, the elements of trust, mutuality and reciprocity[112] underpinned this partnership model. As one teacher–educator commented:

> One of the first impressions that I had about the [activity] was how collegiately it was developed and how people were able to negotiate different elements of the program, like the draft was presented and then

---

112 Kruger et al. 2009

discussed. I thought there was a real genuine sincerity around how this might best serve both universities which had different cohorts in the sense they come from different areas, and how they might get the most out of the program as they have different expectations of them in their settings. (Teacher–Educator, *Reconceptualising Rocks*, 2015)

Collaborative partnerships require the coordination of respective schedules and timetables, and synchronising and integrating the activities and responsibilities of the various partners can be difficult. The willingness to adapt activities is paramount. The initial activity design for *Reconceptualising Rocks* was for inter-university collaboration. This proved difficult and, for 2016, we decide to separate students and offer each university a program tailored to their students' particular educative requirements. This had its benefits in that museum staff involved could focus on the needs and educative objectives pertinent to the students from each university. For example, the program for the more mature and confident master-level students factored in a greater level of conceptual interaction with the museum scientists. The difference in the students' backgrounds flowed into the way in which they interacted in the museum setting. This was noted by academics from both universities. This is not to say that mixed undergraduate and postgraduate programs cannot be effective, but they need to be designed to account for the very specific issues that this can create. Tailored programs also enabled more students from each university to take part in the program at one time, facilitating easier management. These changes were made possible by Melbourne Museum staff's capacity to be flexible and creative in their dealings with the universities.

Successful partnerships require the needs and objectives of each stakeholder to be identified, acknowledged and addressed[113]. In all of the activities under Innovation 4, each of the stakeholders – the teacher educators, PSTs and specialist centres – had specific objectives

---

113 Jones et al. 2016

Innovation 4

but shared the aim of remaining skilled in their field and passing their knowledge to others through education. PSTs:

> ... are now becoming active members of a community that has a dual responsibility both to create educational settings in a classroom but also to maintain an awareness of what living science and mathematics looks like. (Professor David Clarke, *Reconceptualising Rocks*, 2016)

In particular, the partnership with Melbourne Museum introduced PSTs and science students to contemporary museum and scientific practices. Access to science collections and to the research scientists provided insights into the process and practice of science and scientists. By familiarising the participants with the current best practice of teaching geology, the *Reconceptualising Rocks* activity supported students to develop their knowledge of current pedagogical approaches and to extend their understanding of how to teach earth science in innovative and engaging ways.

The combination of familiarising the students with the geology exhibits at the museum, exposure to the science research behind the scenes, and participation in an excursion taken by a passionate expert, provided the students with the knowledge, capability and confidence to teach geology. In this way, the program could be considered transformative[114].

Although the museum collaboration was used as an exemplar, each of the three collaborations (GTAC, Discovery Centre, Melbourne Museum) found that linking universities with science centres in the teaching of PSTs benefited PSTs as they felt more competent and confident to teach and gained a better understanding of how science-related to everyday life. Science centre staff gained a better understanding of how students learn and the teaching process, facilitating better communication. The actual science centres facilitated a better rapport with future teachers. Universities benefited by improving access to the

---

[114] Clarke 2016

science centre resources and knowledge, and participating schools received the teaching resources produced. Thus, collaborations with science centres in the teaching program are to be encouraged and have proven a win-win for all participants.

Conclusion

Key learnings from the ReMSTEP specialist science centre partnerships

One of the key objectives of the ReMSTEP model was to create links by connecting students with contemporary practices in the learning and teaching of science through innovative and engaging pedagogical approaches. These activities introduced students to:

- the practice of scientists
- the process of science
- the role of the specialist centre in supporting contemporary science.

One of the measures of the success of this initiative was the extent to which each of those stakeholder groups felt that their objectives were met and that there was a feeling of value in having participated in the program.

Effective collaborations such as the Melbourne Museum activity, the Discovery Centre partnership and the GTAC collaboration can assist scientists in communicating their craft and, in turn, scientists can assist educators (and would-be-educators) to keep abreast of contemporary science and how it fits within society. However, whether objectives are shared or convergent, if the collaboration is to be successful, there are associated constraints that must be managed. These constraints include: logistics, availability of scientists and centre staff, university course structures, PSTs' commitments that can affect the amount of time spent on such activities, flexibility of centres and institutions, the extent to which the various objectives of the stakeholders are aligned, general communication problems and specific communication challenges in helping students to become conversant with new fields of science and learning pedagogies.

Collaborations with science centres geared around research and education can be extremely valuable when training STEM teachers, as we can leverage the significant educational expertise of researchers and science education specialists. Rather than simply being seen as a source of knowledge, they can assist in equipping PSTs and teachers engaging in ongoing professional development with contemporary learning pedagogies, which employ diverse modes and technologies to enliven the teaching of STEM disciplines. At the same time, such programs can provide more opportunities for scientists to communicate their knowledge and experience in a range of contexts. Looking forward, these interactions mean that scientists can assist educators in staying abreast of contemporary science and how it fits within the various aspects of society at all levels in their careers.

Chapter 8

Innovation 5—Exploring models of interaction between scientists and PSTs

Peta White, Russell Tytler, Stuart Palmer

Introduction

In response to concerns about school students' decreasing engagement with STEM subjects and pathways, and evidence of diminishing comparative performance of Australian students in mathematics and science learning, there has been increasing interest in fostering direct connections between the STEM professional community (scientists, mathematicians, engineers and ICT professionals) and teachers and students. Underpinning this is a view that school mathematics and science are failing to excite students and engage them in working and thinking scientifically and mathematically, and that schooling practices need to change to better reflect practices within the STEM professions in order to engage students in quality learning. Interest in linking schools with the STEM community is evident internationally[115] and there have been recent attempts to chart, within Australia, the incidence and nature of these burgeoning connections[116].

Deakin University researchers have been active in investigating the links between the scientific community and schools[117]. The evaluation of the impact of the CSIRO Scientists and Mathematicians in

---

115   Marginson et al. 2013
116   e.g. Office of the Chief Scientist, 2016
117   Tytler et al. 2015; Tytler et al. 2016; Tytler et al. 2011; Tytler et al. 2008

Schools program (SMiS), in which Tytler and colleagues[118] identified a distinct and significant set of knowledges that STEM professionals could bring to teachers and students, included:

1. modelling of passion and curiosity and what it means to work and think scientifically and mathematically
2. knowledge of STEM workplace practices
3. exemplifying the relevance of STEM in a variety of workplaces.

Teachers in these partnerships reported significant learning and changes to practice, as well as student engagement and learning. However, only a minority of either primary or secondary teachers of mathematics and science are involved in such partnerships or think about how to incorporate contemporary STEM practices into their classrooms. Hence, ReMSTEP has offered the opportunity to explore ways to link PSTs with inspiring models of STEM research and development, to illustrate how these can be translated into school activities, and to offer models of how they, as teachers, might interact with the STEM community.

Within this broad intention, *Innovation 5* has explored a range of models through which PSTs can interact with the STEM research and development community. Mostly this has involved interactions with scientists, reflecting difficulties we have found in finding mathematical researchers willing to explore the translation of their work into school curriculum activities. Some of the activities within ReMSTEP sat within more than one innovation and some that involve direct interaction with scientists are reported in other chapters. These include:

- The development of an undergraduate unit, *Multidisciplinary Science and Technology in Education (MSTE)*, in which students interact with research scientists at a number of levels to explore, through a staged series of assessments, the different audiences

---

[118] Tytler et al. 2015

they communicate with. It was found these close encounters with scientists' practice changed student views of the 'nature of science'.

- Incorporating an activity into an undergraduate unit—*Communicating Science*—where a practising scientist presented their research and students were challenged to develop a communication for school students based on this.

- *Reconceptualising Rocks*: a cross-university activity where PSTs interacted with museum scientists on a geology excursion and explored the research practices and purposes of museum scientists. Students produced a media artefact interpreting this work for school students (see *Innovation 4*).

This chapter focuses on a subset of *Innovation 5* activities in order to explore the affordances of different models of interaction, and the potential of these approaches to interactions to lead to students generally receiving effective learning and dispositional change with regards to contemporary science . The activities are:

- *Stem Cell Exploration*: PSTs working with scientists to produce VCE biology teaching and learning sequences (and other resources focused on VCE biology—such as resources to support conducting investigations and fieldwork)[119].

- *Multimedia resources for biology and environmental education*: PSTs interview a scientist as part of the development of a multimedia resource exemplifying a biology concept or environmental issue (using digiexplanation strategies and sometimes animations)[120].

- *Institute of Frontier Materials (IFM) research practices video-supported activity modules*: Representing the practices of scientists

---

119   http://contemporaryvcebiology.com
120   http://contemporaryvcebiology.com

at the IFM generated by teacher educators and trialled with teachers and PSTs[121].

- *Contemporary Science Workshops*: Groups of PSTs, teachers and teacher educators worked with a scientist to translate their research into school activities. These workshops extended the partnership with the *Advancing Science by Enhancing Learning in the Laboratory* (ASELL) for Schools—Victorian Node project to generate laboratory learning activities that more directly represent contemporary scientific practices (science inquiry skills) and scientists (science as human endeavour)[122].

Other *Innovation 5* activities not reported on in detail but referred to in the text include:

1. IFM Chemistry Education activity—this paralleled the biology multimedia activity, except that one-on-one pairing between PSTs and postgraduate science researchers from the highly productive IFM electro-chemistry unit was expedited by the lecturer, following a forum in which the researchers presented on the nature of and rationale for their research. The resource in this case extended to designing school activities.

2. Environmental science teaching and learning sequences activity—groups of PSTs work with a teacher–educator and a scientist to translate the contemporary science/research into school-based teaching and learning sequences.

3. A ReMSTEP/ASELL for Schools—Victorian Node project: science and education faculty staff work with teachers and scientists to workshop practical activities that exemplify contemporary science, inquiry and representation practices. The ASELL for Schools—Victorian Node team worked to create or refine laboratory activities that represented STEM professionals' stories

---

121 https://blogs.deakin.edu.au/remstep
122 https://blogs.deakin.edu.au/asell-for-schools-vic

generated in the ReMSTEP activities.

The aim of *Innovation 5* is to explore a range of these models of interaction to address the following questions:

- What interactions between PSTs and STEM researchers are productive?
- What aspects of contemporary STEM practice should be focused on in these interactions and in the curriculum?
- What changed teacher practices and school activities are envisaged, and enabled, through these interactions?
- What are the challenges in embedding these links into teacher education?
- What are the payoffs for PSTs, teacher educators and science researchers?
- What potential do these models have to inform school system innovation to better represent contemporary STEM practices?

Exploring models of interaction

These *Innovation 5* activities are framed within a model represented by Figure 8.1, which identifies three broad categories of participants involved in the interactions: STEM professionals who might be science researchers, museum scientists or postgraduate researchers; STEM educators who might be teacher educators, teachers or science centre staff, and PSTs whose role may vary depending on the activity. The model emphasises the multiple ways these three groups might interact, and the variety of outcomes including assessment products and public resources.

As a result of this suite of *Innovation 5* activities, a number of outcomes have been achieved or are in an advanced state of being achieved. These include:

Innovation 5

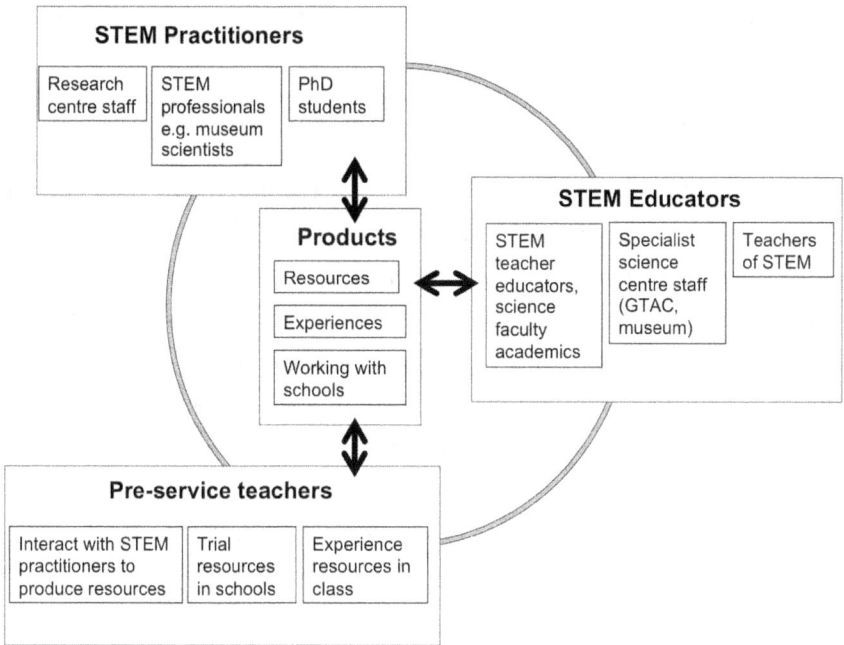

Figure 8.1: A generalised model of interactions under Innovation 5 activities. Source: ReMSTEP 2018

- a set of school activities representing contemporary scientific practices

- a set of teacher education activities to consider ways of incorporating contemporary science into school curricula

- new understandings, for teachers, PSTs, educators and scientists, of the process of translating contemporary scientific practices into the curriculum

- online materials illustrating contemporary science curriculum activities

- knowledge of what works, for PSTs and teachers translating contemporary STEM research and development practices into the school curriculum.

Narrative examples: Four interactions

Stem cell exploration

PSTs from a postgraduate curriculum studies unit in biology were asked if they might be interested in volunteering to work with a scientist to develop teaching and learning materials. Three PSTs offered and, not surprisingly in a cohort of postgraduates, all three had several years' experience in medical research and science practice. When they were matched with an experienced scientist who also had a passion for science communication and with two education academics who were eager to infuse contemporary pedagogy, a productive synergy resulted.

The scientist's passion for communication was made clear in the following quote:

> If anyone is interested in finding out about stem cells, it can be a real challenge. There is a lot of information available online. But a lot of it is either over-hyped, very simplistic and you even see this in the media. A lot of people draw their information from the media. We have to go well beyond the media and get behind the headlines. In this project, we have tried to arm both teachers and students with a more reliable source of information. (Scientist, *Stem Cell Exploration*, 2016)

Coincidentally, the real work on this teaching and learning sequence started at the same time the new study design for the biology curriculum[123] was released. This study design infused understandings about stem cells into key understandings about cell differentiation (rather than stem cell research as an example of gene technology). Sequence one (of the two sequences) focused entirely on the key learning outcomes. The new study design generated considerable interest in the stem cell teaching and learning sequences, as there was now a need for educational materials in the field.

---

[123] VCAA 2015

Another coincidence occurred as the education academics had already begun working on contemporary pedagogies exploring stem cell research as a controversial issue. The use of drama pedagogies to explore issues that might involve many varied positions (or stakeholders) is well regarded[124] yet it was serendipitous that the research projects overlapped enough for ideas to transfuse. Sequence two was developed to scaffold students to explore the issues around stem cell research through whole-class drama pedagogy.

The benefits of this project for the PSTs included:

> For me coming into teaching and deciding to change my career that was in the real world of science it was important for me to get involved in this project because it could link my worlds. It could link my world of science, where I was dealing each day with the latest technology, into the education world. (PST, *Stem Cell Exploration*, 2016)

> Working in this project has given me a greater understanding of curriculum planning, the work of scientists and the back work of teachers—what they do behind the scenes. Our scientist brought so much knowledge and passion about her field and how we can make it relevant in the classroom. The relevance of the science was really exciting. (PST, *Stem Cell Exploration*, 2016)

PSTs were asked what has this project done for them and their teaching? They responded:

> I look at prescribed curriculum differently as I now think that there is a lot more flexibility in there to teach creatively, to go on tangents and to explore the scientific skills outside the key knowledge. (PST, *Stem Cell Exploration*, 2016)

> Working with people who have long and different experiences in

---

124 Curtis et al. 2014

education has been great. The connections I've made within this project and beyond Deakin have given me insight and resources I will use in the future. (PST, *Stem Cell Exploration*, 2016)

Trying to understand how others will approach teaching this material has been really good to help us consider how to present the material. (PST, *Stem Cell Exploration*, 2016)

The PSTs were involved in delivering a workshop introducing the new teaching and learning sequences at a STAV VCE Biology conference. They were also involved in the production of the resource as a website. Video footage was generated to facilitate the online material and all were involved[125].

During the following year, subsequent PSTs enrolled in the same unit were given an opportunity to undertake a similar project (to design a teaching and learning sequence based on the work of a scientist and with support of that scientist). Four students took up this alternative assessment offering. Their topics included: introduced species, immunotherapy, mosquito-borne diseases and responding to antigens. They each enjoyed slightly different experiences, yet all resulted in high-quality and well-resourced sequences[126].

Multimedia resources for biology and environmental education

PSTs were asked to consider a concept from the curriculum and to design a five-minute multimedia explanation that included an interview with a scientist that would help explain the concept by offering an example of the scientist's current research. The 'digiexplanation'[127] is a pedagogical strategy that engages students in learning by explaining and communicating science through multimedia development.

---

[125] http://contemporaryvcebiology.com/stem-cells
[126] http://contemporaryvcebiology.com
[127] http://www.digiexplanations.com

The PSTs needed to choose the right kind of concept—one that could link to contemporary research and came from the curriculum. They then had to find a scientist who was interested and available. They had several aspects to manage and it often required high-level skills to conduct the interview so that useful product resulted.

> This is an excellent activity to learn new concepts in biology. In order to produce the [multimedia explanation], you really have to unpack the concept to make sure that you understand it before you can scaffold the video. In a previous [multimedia explanation], that I produced, the topic was very unfamiliar to me and producing the [multimedia explanation] really helped me to understand the topic and why it is important to understand. (PST, *Multimedia resources for biology and environmental education*, 2016)

After choosing the concept and researching it enough to generate deep understandings, PSTs knew which scientists they could invite to interview and what to ask them if they agreed. PSTs also had to consider technology tools and applications to generate the multimedia explanation.

> This activity allowed me to engage with new technologies and to think about how I can incorporate them into my classroom. It has also given me new ideas about how to design assessments for my students. It has encouraged me to think outside the box and give my students some more creative freedom in their assessments. (PST, *Multimedia resources for biology and environmental education*, 2016)

The challenges faced by PSTs related to the decisions they had to make about how to represent the content so that they communicated clearly.

> It was a great way to look into the contemporary science that is out there and was a fun way to create a resource that can be used for

students. It was hard to put a concept into a five-minute video, but it made you seek out the correct information you wanted to get across. (PST, *Multimedia resources for biology and environmental education*, 2016)

I think one of the best aspects of the [multimedia explanation] is that it forces you to think about why you are teaching a topic/concept. It brings relevance to the curriculum both for the teachers and the students. Sometimes teaching science can feel like you are just regurgitating the curriculum. Producing a [multimedia explanation] brings perspective. (PST, *Multimedia resources for biology and environmental education*, 2016)

PSTs indicated a greater realisation of scientists' work and a changed view of their capability to craft engaging curriculum resources around contemporary science.

Using multimedia to teach science is certainly an interesting way to engage students. It is important to be able to make your own resources, as those out there are often not suited to exactly what you need. (PST, *Multimedia resources for biology and environmental education*, 2016)

I had never considered the ease or importance of getting my friends from the scientific community to help me explain concepts. (PST, *Multimedia resources for biology and environmental education*, 2016)

A resource to use for the future and an exemplar of my work for future potential employers. A strong understanding of copyright law. (PST, *Multimedia resources for biology and environmental education*, 2016)

It's great to be able to show students the type of interesting work they could get into if they want to continue in the science pathway by giving them an insight into their work. (PST, *Multimedia resources for biology and environmental education*, 2016)

Innovation 5

The PSTs were scaffolded in the assessment design in that once they had a concept and scientists, they had to design a storyboard that detailed what, how and when they would generate their multimedia explanation—the technical aspects. Figure 8.2 is an example of a PST-generated storyboard.

Figure 8.2: The storyboard for developing the multimedia explanation.
Source: ReMSTEP 2018

Once the storyboard was generated it was shared among peers and a formal review was conducted resulting in each PST receiving up to three peer reviews critiquing their work. PSTs found that this layer of feedback helped them improve the multimedia explanation considerably.

The storyboard offered above led to a high-quality multimedia explanation (see Figure 8.3).

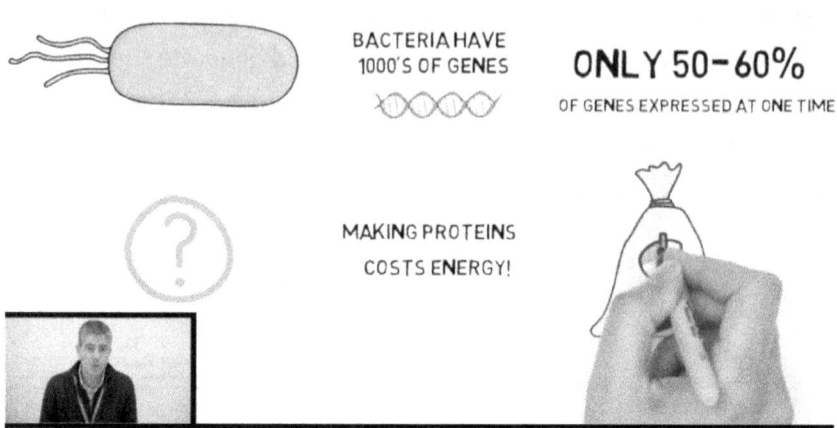

Figure 8.3: An example of a multimedia resource,[128] several multimedia explanations have been presented.[129] Source: ReMSTEP 2018

Institute for Frontier Materials (IFM) research practices video-supported activity modules

Our approach to *Innovation 5* was to, wherever relevant, engage with the broader discipline range of STEM, with contemporary/cutting-edge STEM, and with STEM in a wider societal context. A key opportunity to realise these aims at Deakin was to engage with IFM, which is a world-leading institute undertaking research and development in modern materials. IFM's annual budget is directed to research projects that are roughly split equally between discovery research and applied/translation research. IFM have an education/outreach mandate, so collaborating with IFM was a mutually beneficial and productive way to access a working, cutting-edge environment and people that authentically represented the complementary aspects of science and engineering: theory and practice, invention and innovation, research and development (R&D), and discovery and application.

---

128 https://video.deakin.edu.au/media/t/0_nlpyjjr6
129 http://contemporaryvcebiology.com

Innovation 5 121

As part of its R&D work in a range of materials fields, IFM has extensive resources devoted to carbon fibre reinforced polymer (CFRP) composite materials. CFRPs combine the lightweight and high tensile strength of carbon fibre with the strength and rigidity of a polymer resin. The resulting 'composite' material is extremely strong relative to its weight and is an excellent example of a modern material. Its creation combines fundamental materials science directed at improving the properties of the component materials, and applied engineering directed to improving the properties of the resultant composite material via optimising the production process. These are some of the STEM processes related to chemistry and materials properties, forces, mathematical modelling, structure, scientific R&D processes, and science as a human endeavour we wish to represent in the school curriculum,.

While most of our projects within *Innovation 5* involve direct interactions between PSTs, scientists and educators, we recognised a problem with the scalability of such approaches. Similarly, while it is possible to engage PSTs directly with the materials, processes, science and engineering of CFRP production, it is more difficult to translate this into understandable, safe and inexpensive learning activities that might be undertaken in classes. In the IFM activity, we sought to produce digital resources that would convey the essential elements of the practice of contemporary R&D in authentic and engaging ways.

To represent the personal, human aspect of the practice of modern R&D, we interviewed a number of scientists and engineers from IFM about their work, addressing questions such as:

- Can you introduce yourself and a bit about your history?

- Can you explain in simple terms the main research project that you are working on?

- How did the main research question behind your research come about?

- How is your research work funded?

- How do you hope/think that the outcomes of your research will be used?

- What inspired you to be a researcher?

Separately, we interviewed the Director of IFM and a research project leader, to explore questions related to the makeup of IFM's workforce, how the various research programs are initiated, how IFM and its work is funded, who are the research partners that work with IFM, and how IFM compares with similar institutes around the world. We arranged for the these interviews to be filmed professionally for future use. The videos[130] included a balance of gender and undergraduate STEM backgrounds, and a range of the materials R&D undertaken at IFM.

We interviewed one of the researchers, Matt Jennings, in more detail. Matt's PhD studies were an investigation into how heating rates during the curing (setting) of the composite resin in the production of a carbon-fibre sandwich beam affected the strength of the completed beam structure. We filmed a range of questions and responses, including the purpose of his work, the science underlying it and his personal perspectives on working as a materials scientist. The video artefacts thus obtained, representing different aspects of the operation of a modern R&D institute, could be used in many productive ways. As stand-alone videos, they provide insights into issues including:

1. the nature and importance of modern materials

2. what drives a materials R&D institutes like IFM

3. the 'science as a human endeavour' aspects of Matt's experience and purposes.

By deliberately selecting interview subjects and the stimulus questions used, our intention was to capture perspectives from high-level organisational drivers through to the detailed activities of individual researchers. Throughout all levels, we hoped to represent aspects of

---

130   https://blogs.deakin.edu.au/remstep/researchers-videos

contemporary STEM R&D practices—how are science, technology, engineering and mathematics combined in the real world?

The team brainstormed ways to develop low-cost classroom activities based on readily available materials that secondary students could complete, and that would both represent the R&D work undertaken by researchers at IFM, and demonstrate some of the STEM principles underpinning that work. Drawing inspiration from the PhD research of Matt Jennings, we developed a number of potential activities. One was making a composite panel from expanded polystyrene foam bonded with cloth tape—applying cloth tape with high tensile strength length-wise around a foam panel dramatically increases its stiffness and resistance to bending. A second was a method for producing an expanded honeycomb structure from recycled A4 copy paper using PVA glue—the result was a lightweight, low-density, high-strength structural element representative of the filler material used in many CFRP composite panels made commercially.

The research team managed the development of the videos and initial experimental activities. To engage PSTs (and others), and to develop and document additional learning activities representing contemporary R&D practices, we organised a workshop day. Present on the day were several participants experienced in applying the ASELL for Schools project methodology for prototyping and refining experimental learning activities. We adopted a template for documenting proposed activities based on the ASELL for Schools model. The workshop, following tours of a range of IFM R&D facilities, and a scene-setting presentation, focused on group brainstorming of possible school activities. Within the limits of the participants present, each group contained a researcher, an education academic, an experienced teacher and a PST. Groups worked to propose and/or refine potential learning activities on materials science principles. Subsequently, some of these ideas for activities, and other concepts inspired by the process, have been developed and documented more fully by experienced educators. Additionally, some have been trialled with teachers and refined as part of the ASELL for Schools activity.

From these IFM resources and activities, an online module has been developed consisting of a set of videos and activities, with teacher instructions, that represent and illustrate the work of IFM and its researchers. Alongside the model, we developed teacher education resources to interpret and generate discussion about the module as a possible representation of contemporary STEM R&D in the curriculum.

A number of challenges were encountered in the conceptualisation and development of the module:

- experienced teachers indicated that videos on their own would have limited appeal to students—relevant context would have to be provided

- engaging mathematics researchers and foregrounding the mathematics elements of STEM in such activities remains difficult

- meaningful engagements between the various parties are time consuming and require significant goodwill and negotiation of schedules

- cutting-edge R&D involves complex knowledge and processes—representing these in activities that are engaging, low-cost, practical and safe for the classroom requires careful thought

- cutting-edge R&D is multidisciplinary, so may be difficult to fit neatly into a school curriculum that is already crowded and based on historical divisions between STEM disciplines.

The initial workshop development model described above, including the engagement with the ASELL for Schools project, has been extended to other activities under *Innovation 5*.

Contemporary Science Workshops

Based on the relative success of the stem cell and other controversial issues teaching and learning sequences (*Stem Cell Exploration*) and looking for ways to streamline or scale up the connections of teachers,

PSTs and scientists, the Contemporary Science Workshops were designed. These workshops were hosted on two campuses (Waurn Ponds and Burwood) and were well attended. The ASELL for Schools—Victorian Node project was involved in the workshops and the final product was designed to fit into this project as practical learning activities (laboratory based).

Scientists were invited to participate in a three-hour session. They were asked to attend without materials prepared to maximise flexibility about what aspects of their research were taken up. Teachers were invited to attend a half-day session (with teaching relief covered by the project). PSTs were asked to volunteer for the half-day session (receiving a token gift). Putting these three experts together to develop learning activities was a rewarding move, as many of the participants describe:

> Really worthwhile exercise. One of the reasons the utility and excitement of science does not reach school children is that the teachers of science subjects have never worked in the field i.e. they have not been a biologist, a chemist etc. So, it's a bit like teaching plumbing to someone when you have all the theory but no first-hand experience of going into a house and doing an actual plumbing job. Thus, having a scientist to contribute means that the problem of teachers being disconnected with the science disciplines is solved, at least to some extent. (PST, *Contemporary Science Workshops*, 2016)

> It is always interesting to see which of my findings are generally interesting to others. Also, because I do very little teaching, it is illuminating to learn what approaches teachers think will work best with students. (Scientist, *Contemporary Science Workshop*, 2016)

> To be able to discuss with the scientists and have them explain the research but also to jointly work out how to select an appropriate task to take to the school. Without the experienced teacher, the pre-teacher and the scientist it could never have been achieved. (PST, *Contemporary Science Workshops*, 2016)

> I think students enjoy and perhaps learn best from material that is recent so I would imagine that having new perspectives helps teachers to present concepts in a way that will interest students. (PST, *Contemporary Science Workshops*, 2016)

At each site, we matched teachers and PSTs with scientists. The conversation was initially directed by the scientists who explained their research. Teachers and PSTs asked questions and after about 20 minutes the conversation shifted towards the educators who then started to work the research into practical activities for students from Years 7–10. The curricula connections were sometimes hard to establish, although science as human endeavour and science inquiry skills were well taken up.

The products were variable, with some groups preparing a near-finished product, while others enjoyed a great conversation and planned some activities but nothing much was written and crafted. In some cases, we will initiate further contact with the scientists to explore possible school activities. The successful groups have now developed practical activities ready for workshopping and testing in school situations, although these required additional inputs from educators to develop to this near-complete stage.

Each scientist was interviewed on video. These interviews have been crafted into 5–8-minute productions that provide viewers with an insight into the person the scientist is, their passions for researching in their field, and some insight into the research itself. These products will be useful to augment the final learning activity.

Two examples of the video resources follow.

1. Video of Euan Ritchie relating to the research that was used to develop practical learning experiences[131].

2. Video of Stuart Palmer relating to the research that was used to develop practical learning experiences[132].

---

131 https://video.deakin.edu.au/media/t/0_pajrgn38
132 https://video.deakin.edu.au/media/t/0_q3b7ozl5

Some of these practical activities will be presented on the ASELL for Schools—Victorian Node website[133] and cross-linked to the Deakin ReMSTEP site.

The next step was to take the positive experiences from these workshops and redesign the experience to become a group assessment task in a PST unit. Environmental science teaching and learning sequences were produced through the efforts of a group of undergraduates who had met with a scientist a couple of times over a six-week period. The students scaffolded teaching and learning opportunities as a sequence over 3–5 lessons. They were also asked to produce a multimedia resource to use as part of the teaching and learning sequence. The results were generally positive, although required additional effort to bring them to a publishable level.

We have planned a future project to further develop this process of engaging scientists, teachers and PSTs to produce contemporary science teaching and learning sequences for school students. In this project, scientists will be supported to come to the table with a series of materials already developed: video materials, data in useable formats and narratives constructed about the research questions and context, the data collection strategies and the research findings. The workshop will be for a longer period and will be scaffolded to ensure that near-finished products are completed by the end of the session. This project is being undertaken at Deakin University and was completed by the end of 2017.

Findings and discussion

These *Innovation 5* activities vary across of the following dimensions:

1. The nature of the interaction, from direct one-on-one interaction, interaction between a scientist and a group, sometimes involving teacher or teacher–educator input, or virtual interactions such as with the IFM module.

---

[133] https://blogs.deakin.edu.au/asell-for-schools-vic

2. The extent to which the activity was embedded in a teacher education unit, either as part of the assessment for all students, an optional activity or volunteer PSTs working outside unit assessment.

3. The degree of management of the interaction, from being scripted by the lecturer or organised by the student themselves.

4. The focus, either on resource production or on individual insight and reflective experience of the PST.

5. The time over which the interaction takes place, from one interaction through to extended consultation during resource development.

Thus, the *Stem Cell Exploration* activity involved direct interaction of scientifically research-experienced PSTs with a leading scientist to produce school resources, in collaboration with a biology educator and an arts educator. In the multimedia explanations, students recruited a scientist and worked on developing a multimedia resource to clarify a science concept relevant to the senior biology or science curriculum.

The different activities are conceived of as a staged process, in some cases the interaction with PSTs leading to exemplar resources that form the basis of teacher education activities discussing possible interactions with contemporary science. Figure 8.4 shows the different models of interaction between scientists, PSTs and educators that were explored, and the types of outcomes and resources that resulted.

1. For the *Communicating Science*/IFM chemistry activities, the materials produced were for within-unit assessment purposes and aided reflection on scientific practices and how they might be translated.

2. The second model involving scientist and PST interactions leading to resources for schools, exemplified by the multimedia explanations and *Reconceptualising Rocks,* showed how generating explanations using digital technologies is a creative and engaging

pedagogical strategy. Additionally, the multimedia explanations can be useful as resources for teachers and PSTs, and some have been selected for further development and website publication.

3. For the stem cells activity, PSTs with experience in medical research fields worked with teacher educators and senior scientists to produce web materials for use in schools, and also in teacher education.

4. Finally, IFM and the ReMSTEP/ASELL for Schools—Victorian Node activities, and the Contemporary Science Workshops where scientists, PSTs, teachers and teacher educators worked together in various combinations to produce resources for schools that act as the basis for further teacher education activities.

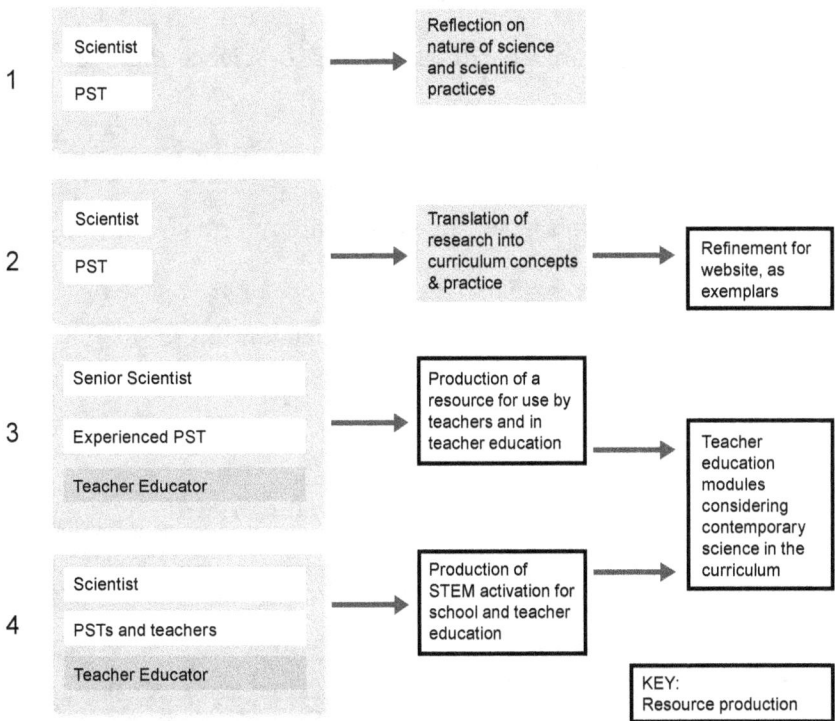

Figure 8.4: Resource production models for the Innovation 5 activities.
Source: ReMSTEP 2018

Findings regarding outcomes

Outcomes for the different stakeholders have been discussed in the individual activity descriptions above, but Table 8.1 shows the percentage of 'agree' and 'strongly agree' responses to three key questions from 2016 online surveys, across the biology multimedia explanation, the parallel IFM *Communicating Science* activity, and the *Reconceptualising Rocks* museum activity. The results are strong, particularly for knowledge gains. In some cases, students claimed they did not gain new insights into scientists' practice because they already had experience working as researchers.

From these and other evaluation data (interviews, focus groups) we can make general statements about the success of these activities for PSTs, in that they:

- enjoyed interacting with scientists
- often gained new insights into the nature of science and scientists' practice
- often gained new perspectives on scientists as people
- acquired ideas on how to represent contemporary science in the curriculum
- learned new and important science understandings.

From the activity I gained new insights into scientists' research and development practices and roles	83%
From the activity I learnt some interesting science concepts	86%
From the activity I was engaged in new and interesting approaches to teaching science	79%

Table 8.1: The percentage of 'agree' and 'strongly agree' responses to three key questions from 2016 online surveys

There were positive benefits for the scientists also, in that they generally gained:

- insights into how their work might translate into the curriculum
- experience in communicating their research to the public.

The latter is an important finding in that scientists are keen to have their postgraduate researchers interpret their research for PSTs. This gives postgraduate students experience and clarity in communicating the purposes and public relevance of their research.

Challenges for models of interaction

While contemporary science is often represented in science textbooks as 'modern applications', individual schools and teachers do not often entertain the idea of drawing on local scientists and cutting-edge research. This is due to practicalities such as lack of time and/or knowledge, or histories of practice relying on textbooks. ReMSTEP offered a proving ground for examining how PSTs and teachers can productively engage with the STEM research community, and the conditions under which contemporary ideas can translate into school activities. Certainly, with the 'science as a human endeavour' strand of the curriculum, we are encouraged to represent scientists and their practices in school science activity.

Through observing interactions, interviews and survey responses we identified a number of challenges, possible solutions and general principles for translating contemporary scientific practices into school activities.

1. For some contemporary scientific research and development practice, and scientists' experiences, there were difficulties with determining just what should be the focus when translating this into school activities. While often the translation was non-problematic, where the science was abstract or complex and did not immediately suggest an interesting entrée for activities, or where

the understanding of the PST did not allow easy entry into the science, a number of strategies were adopted, including:

- The conceptual principle underpinning the research was translated to devise activities exploring a simpler but related phenomenon. An example would be translating property parameters into simpler parameters, and testing procedures of composite materials into testing of everyday materials. In that case, the scientist's story became the backdrop to, and justification for, more traditional inquiry investigations.

- The scientists did not automatically know what to present from their practice that would be appropriate for translation. Many learned to put more emphasis on the broad framing and social purposes of their research, including economic and/or environmental constraints or aims, rather than simply focusing on theoretical abstractions.

- It was useful to have teachers and/or education academics working with PSTs and scientists to explore the translation process, to make judgments about what would engage students, and what learning to focus on.

- Sometimes where the details of contemporary ideas did not suggest an engaging story for school students, the broad story of how the science was practised sometimes took precedence, such as focusing on discussions of the role of mathematical modelling in systematically investigating new materials, rather than on details of the models as such, which could be quite abstract.

2. In some cases, it was difficult to find science understanding curriculum outcomes at the appropriate level to match the ideas underpinning the scientific practice. At times, it was helpful to also look at the technology curriculum, science inquiry or science as human endeavour outcomes. A flexible approach to curriculum outcomes is sometimes needed to take advantage of what scientists have to offer.

3. The interactions of PSTs with scientists depended to some extent on the maturity and experience of the PST. Unsupported interactions between undergraduate PSTs sometimes led to superficial exploration of the scientist's work. In general, more structure needs to be provided for undergraduate students.

4. In all interactions, questions of time and rewards for both parties needed to be considered. In some activities involving postgraduate (and experienced) volunteer PSTs undertaking work with senior scientists, there was considerable commitment and investment of conceptual resources. For interactions that were part of unit assessment, the rewards were sufficient for attention to the task and time could be found, sometimes with support in interactions with the scientists.

What have we learned?

A number of key learnings concerning the representation of science practices in school curricula have come from this suite of projects:

1. There are significant benefits for PSTs and teachers in interacting with scientists in terms of their understandings of the contemporary relevance of scientific work, the nature of scientists' practice, and sharpening their knowledge.

2. There are benefits in bringing together scientists, teacher educators, PSTs and teachers to undertake the translation process—translation is not straightforward and within these wider groupings there is a need for 'brokerage' across the scientific and education cultures.

3. Insights have been developed into how to manage PST–scientist interactions within a number of models that can be extended more widely. Insights have also been developed into varied strategies for translating scientists' knowledge and practice into worthwhile school activities.

4. Interesting and innovative school activities arising from teacher–scientist partnerships often involve combinations of the STEM disciplines, and industry relevance.

5. The translation of contemporary practices into schools depends on teachers having a flexible view of the curriculum.

6. The experience is educative for the scientists who need to learn how to communicate key aspects and wider significance of their work, as well as to be flexible in responding to pedagogical needs.

7. In the process of these explorations, education and science engineering researchers developed productive relations. We have learnt the value on both sides for these cross-disciplinary links, and collaborations are ongoing.

Conclusion

What remains to be learned? What are possible ways forward?

The ReMSTEP experience has broken significant new ground in exploring different arrangements by which scientists can partner with educators, and contemporary scientific practice can be represented in the school curriculum. The program offers a model for transforming the school mathematics and science curriculum through increasing its relevance and representing the thinking and working of STEM professionals and the critical role of STEM in society. The program is thus a pilot of what could be a significant circuit breaker for STEM in schools. There are, however, important questions to explore if we are to build a scalable model around bringing contemporary STEM practice into schools.

1. How can we link schools, teachers and scientists in scalable ways?

2. What are the key knowledges and experiences that scientists need to emphasise, and bring into school curriculum experiences?

3. How can teachers and STEM professionals be supported to make the most of interactions and to be clear about the principles on which partnership activities need to be based?

4. What are the advantages of having the scientist interact with students or teachers? Can we meaningfully represent scientific practice virtually; for example, through video or via text and images?

5. How can STEM industries be productively involved in STEM education partnership activities in a scalable way?

6. What are the implications of this work for the way STEM subject curricula are framed and enacted?

Chapter 9

Innovations 6 & 7—Building the pipeline: Recruiting high-potential mathematics and science teachers and leveraging existing student expertise

David Hoxley, James Stratford, Nick Tran, Peter Cox

Introduction

A key factor affecting the quality of STEM education is the short supply of teachers with the necessary levels of expertise. This problem is made worse when teachers have minimal subject-matter expertise; for example, having completed as little as one subject at tertiary level. In 2016, the Australian Council for Educational Research (ACER), using data from the Staff in Australia's Schools (SiAS) survey[134], reported that at least one in five teachers of mathematics and science at Years 7–10 are working out-of-field. The flow-on effect of this is seen in undergraduate performance. For example, in 2014 at one Melbourne metropolitan university, almost one-third of students enrolled in first-year physics failed to pass. While other factors would have contributed, this can, at least in part, be seen as evidence of weak foundations, unable to be strengthened by teachers whose own experience of mathematics and science may be limited.

Innovations 6 & 7 sought to attend to the supply shortage of teachers with deep subject matter expertise in mathematics and sciences, especially physics, ICT, geography and data science. The approaches used are linked by an emphasis on engaging emerging teachers with experience of science as practised by scientists, rather than stockpiling discipline-specific facts and procedures.

It is perhaps useful to look at *Innovations 6 & 7* in reverse order. Indeed, these innovations are really a secondary outcome of all the activities making up ReMSTEP. When the proceeding innovations are aligned with each other, as a deliberate consequence, better-prepared STEM teachers will flow between universities, schools and other workplaces.

Innovation 7: Building a recruitment pipeline of high-potential mathematics and science teachers

Our aim for the activities of *Innovation 7* was to increase the size of the pool of teaching students with specialist knowledge by recruiting undergraduate students with relevant majors. To this end, several programs were tasked with raising undergraduates' awareness of teaching careers and providing additional support for these students as they progressed from teacher training to full-time teaching. The logic behind this approach is clear; students who already demonstrate a solid grasp of discipline foundations are better equipped to make the most of additional specialist training from mathematics and science teaching professionals.

The real strength of each of the *Innovation 7* activities was how they provided high-performing undergraduate mathematics and science students with first-hand experience of, and direct engagement with, teaching in primary and secondary schools. Additionally, participating in designing learning activities gives these high-potential students tangible evidence of their value and the types of contributions they can make, even at this early stage in their careers.

Some students who succeed at senior levels of mathematics and science have received more support and inspiration from outside school, such as from family members. This may explain why scientists' perceptions of mathematics and science teachers are often negative[135]. Working with excellent teaching professionals exposes such students to new and more engaging ways of teaching, allowing them to reset their preconceptions regarding the identity of teachers.

The following sections outline some key activities and identify ways in which they addressed *Innovation 7*.

Schools Science Project

The *Schools Science Project* (SSP) generated two resources: a new science undergraduate unit (SCI3910) and an interactive website, *Monash Science Squad* (MSS).

In the undergraduate unit, science students further developed employability skills through a placement in a school. Each student was required to research, develop, manage and teach a science-based module that matched the learning outcomes specified by their supervising teacher. Prior to their school placement, students participated in a series of workshops on understanding and catering for different learning styles, motivation, team work, goal setting, planning, management, leadership, effective communication and presentation skills, asking the right questions and reflecting.

The MSS is a platform that supports school students' engagement with science. Primary school students can use the platform to reflect on and ask questions about science activities they encounter outside their normal classroom program. Most of the learning we observed took place outside of school during evenings and weekends or over school holidays; for example, through visits to museums, parks and discovery centres. The website design was intended for parents to support their children's learning by overseeing these activities. Participating children could record their science-related learning experiences on the website. Volunteer undergraduate science students monitored the site, answered questions and gave appropriate feedback.

There have been mutual benefits for members of both the education

---

[135] Taylor et al. 2008

and science faculties, especially the sharing of insights across diverse projects, and the sharing of expert knowledge and resources. A number of participating science students were motivated to consider taking up one of the available pathways to teaching as a career, with some science students who initially intended to become secondary teachers changing their focus to careers in primary education (as schools participating in the subject were all primary schools). Science undergraduates who participated in the activities were impressed by the science education approaches modelled, and often commented that they had poor experiences of science in schools as learners. It became clear that their experience in learning science had too much emphasis on content. They responded to and applied the notion of enquiry-based learning and collaborative learning in a true sense. The schoolteachers involved gained much in terms of professional development, particularly in terms of enquiry-based learning, collaboration, dialogic teaching and contextualised experiences. They were keen to pursue more extensive collaboration outside the unit.

AMSPP partnerships: ASELL, GTP, FARLabs and In2science

Projects were conducted in partnership with four activities initiated under the AMSPP[136], in order to enhance the ways in which undergraduate and postgraduate science students engage with schools. AMSPP projects were commissioned by the Office of the Chief Scientist to connect secondary school students and teachers with cutting-edge science and scientists[137]. The three activities were *Advancing Science by Enhancing Learning in the Laboratory* (ASELL), *Growing Tall Poppies* (GTP), Freely Accessible Remote Laboratories (FARLabs) and In2science. ReMSTEP leveraged these existing programs, where possible incorporating mathematics and science PSTs into their activities, so they could gain experience in the intersection of secondary school science education with university research environments.

---

136   AMSPP
137   Office of the Chief Scientist 2012b

The ASELL activities involve using carefully curated workshops to develop engaging and accessible classroom laboratory experiments for wider use[138]. The way that ReMSTEP involved PSTs is described in Chapter 5 (p. 61). What is of interest here is the involvement of postgraduate students from IFM in developing the highly successful composite materials activity and participating in workshop activities alongside school students, teachers and PSTs.

The program also yielded other significant benefits. ASELL provided an opportunity for academic staff from both the education and science faculties at Deakin University to work closely with each other. While the program focused on raising the awareness of students by collaborating with industry professionals and scientists (including postgraduate students), it also reported significant changes in pedagogies of inquiry-based learning.

The GTP[139] program places small groups of female, and regional middle-year students (male and female) in the research environment of a physics department where they conduct and evaluate research projects in partnership with postgraduate students (who represent early-career scientists) and senior academic staff. ReMSTEP incorporated PSTs in the intensive three-day program. The PSTs participated in the activities with the school students, observing the way the scientists transmitted contemporary science at the various levels, and where appropriate acting as facilitators. Most high school students taking part reported that the program gave them exposure to material that they would otherwise not have had, and they reported increased motivation to pursue science into senior high school and at the tertiary level.

FARLabs[140] provides a remote hands-on experience of manipulating and controlling real lab-based experiments, focused on nuclear physics. FARLabs is also an example of a program that can be delivered to rural and remote communities as well as schools that lack the

---

138   ASELL Schools
139   Growing Tall Poppies
140   FARLabs

necessary infrastructure or expertise to run dedicated labs. Support from ReMSTEP allowed it to continue operating beyond its initial funding to serve as an online e-laboratory for PSTs and teachers of physics and general science to use in their teaching practice. FARLabs was used as part of the GTP program and was observed to be a useful catalyst for shared metacognitive reflection between postgraduate scientists, PSTs and school students. It also reflects the increasing use of tele-presence and remote operation in contemporary scientific practice[141]. The FARLabs program has been received enthusiastically with over 53 PSTs and in-service teachers signing up in 2016 alone. This usage is likely to continue to grow over time.

In2science[142] trains undergraduate science students to be volunteer peer mentors in Years 8–9 mathematics and science classes. Working across several universities, ReMSTEP drew on existing experience to explore the potential of In2science for recruiting science undergraduate students to the possibility of teaching careers. While In2science is effective in allowing interested science undergraduates to explore the classroom in a low-pressure environment, the voluntary nature arguably attracts students who had already considered teaching as a pathway. The impact of In2science could be improved by embedding it in the fabric of all universities in a stable, ongoing manner.

By actively participating in the teaching process and communicating the science that they are engaged in to young students, both science undergraduates and higher-degree research students were given the opportunity to increase their own level of capability in ways that have clear value both in teaching specifically and in their professional lives more generally. While most participants still believed that they would pursue a career in science, thanks to having the chance to wear the teacher's hat as a mentor, many expressed their willingness to consider teaching as a real option.

---

141 Kennepohl et al. 2006
142 In2science

Science Students in Schools

In the *Science Students in Schools/Science in Schools* unit, science postgraduate students undertook a placement at Albert Park College, a school into which the Gene Technology Access Centre (GTAC) provides outreach programs. Before beginning their placements, students received assistance from GTAC staff in developing their capability to work with school students. This included assistance developing inclusive questioning techniques and facilitating interaction in a classroom setting. During the actual placement, experienced teachers worked with the undergraduate students to share their teaching expertise. The resulting learning, reflection and synthesis of the science graduate students' placement experience were central to a professional skills subject contributing to their MSc degree. This program is described in Chapter 2 (p. 13).

At GTAC, graduate students reported camaraderie and connectedness with the science educators. Similarly, at Albert Park College the school was enthusiastic in their support of the next generation of educators, which contributed to making participants feel welcome and supported as future teachers.

The science students participating in the program learned about the factors that impact student learning while gaining practical teaching experience. Participants also developed a deeper understanding of the challenges and rewards of contemporary teaching practice. The placement helped them to understand that science education needs to be tailored to the audience, and science teachers need to encourage active learning through well-crafted questions and reflections, rather than just lecturing about a topic. It also highlighted the importance of making science learning interactive, relevant, and engaging: aiming for a balance between science content and the stimulation, which arises from learning. Importantly also, by gaining experience in explaining scientific concepts to the public, and especially young students, participants felt more confident as communicators.

This project tapped into a real appetite for students to work with others who are working at a level of science understanding similar to their own. As a result, requests to work in secondary teaching are much higher. This preference is more indicative that when scientists become educators they are often most keen to get to the 'meaty' end of the science, which often means working with older and more advanced students. As STEM teaching in junior years becomes more engaging for primary and high school students, it is also likely to attract more early-career teachers as well.

Innovation 6: Building on existing student expertise in mathematics and science

Innovation 6 focused on the next stage of the 'pipeline', regarding students in graduate teaching programs. It made the existing body of discipline-specific expertise available to MTeach students via interactions with subject matter experts. In many cases, these were senior undergraduate or postgraduate students, as well as academics and industry experts. The projects had a secondary agenda that aligns with *Innovation 7*, that of recruiting teachers with extensive existing expertise. This is highlighted by the activities described below.

Back to School

In the *Back to School* (B2S) activity, undergraduate mathematics and science students teamed up with pre-service primary or secondary teachers to create enriching activities for primary and secondary school students. The primary aim of this project component was to enable undergraduate mathematics and science students to open their eyes to a teaching career, while also giving PSTs a new perspective on mathematics and science.

By bringing the PSTs and the science undergraduates together, another dimension was added to the overall experience of the undergraduate students. Not only did they experience personally what current-day Australian mathematics and science lessons look like, they were also able to interact with future teachers over the course of the project. The exchange of experiences (and emotions) between the science undergraduates and their respective PSTs was also of great benefit to the undergraduates, who might not be clear what careers they intend to pursue, or who might want to know more about the reality of classroom teaching.

> Normally, teachers are standing up so they are looking down at their students. But the teacher in the class that I observed, he said 'try to get down to the same level with the students'. To me that showed how the teacher could build a closer relationship with the students. It showed me a different perspective than I'm used to and that teaching done differently can be done in a way that makes a difference. That's encouraging to me. (Undergraduate science student, *Back to School*, 2015)

> What I took away from this experience was that when students have to actually think about how to teach someone else they really come to understand what they know and don't know. They actually have to get down to the nuts and bolts of what they are working with in order to be able to teach their fellow students. (PST, *Back to School*, 2015)

Both the undergraduate science students and the PSTs described the experience as 'eye-opening'. During the program, both groups had the opportunity to talk and network with the staff of the placement schools, and some created friendships that will serve them well as they enter the workforce.

> I think it is important that our students in the teacher education programs go through as many experiences as possible before they decide what type of teacher they want to be… The whole experience was about … allowing them to reconceptualise what mathematics and science classrooms across a range of schools are like from when they were students themselves. (Associate Professor Wee Tiong Seah, *Back to School* program organiser, 2015)

By coming 'back to school', the science undergraduates were given the opportunity to see first-hand what mathematics and science lessons can look like, and to experience the sheer joy of interacting with children and seeing them learn and understand. Having seen what school teaching in Australia is like, they have also become potential spokespeople for careers in mathematics and science teaching in their student communities.

All students who were interviewed expressed an intention to become a schoolteacher at some point in their working lives. This feedback is extremely useful as it underscores the more complex ways in which the emerging generation views the nature of their career. People expect to have multiple careers over the course of their working life. This willingness to include teaching as part of the career mix is immensely valuable and needs to be considered when designing the various modes of study and certification necessary to enter the teaching profession.

While most science undergraduate students still aspire to careers in science, this activity also functioned to help students recognise the high demand for *mathematics* teachers in Australia and the consequent employability.

Communicating Science

The *Communicating Science* unit of undergraduate study was designed to build a wider set of capabilities for STEM graduates and included communicating contemporary science for teaching purposes as part of ReMSTEP. Students studying science communication were given the opportunity to attend seminars presented by research fellows, research doctoral students and staff from IFM. This activity included students from a range of backgrounds, enrolled in science, education and engineering courses.

> For me, the best thing was seeing somebody similar to me, someone who was a student, and seeing where their work took them ... and some of the discoveries they were able to make ... nobody else had made those sort of discoveries, so it was really groundbreaking. (Science undergraduate, 2015)

The project model engaged students in groups to produce useful communication artefacts, and at the same time giving meaningful experience and feedback on communication to scientists, in a supportive and familiar environment. The development of this project was informed by theories of authentic learning in teaching and learning[143].

There is evidence that the experience gave many students ideas and confidence for teaching science in schools in the future. A number of the students were recruited into the Successful Students—STEM program[144], which places science and engineering students in science, mathematics and technology classrooms in Geelong secondary schools.

Conclusion

The traditional way of envisaging the *pipeline* feeding students through post-secondary education and into their chosen careers is no longer valid in the way it was only two decades ago. Higher education is no longer seen as a one-off experience leading into a single career. It is increasingly common to return to university or other forms of higher education repeatedly over the course of a working life. Unlike the old pipeline, which was reassuringly linear and concentrated over a short time, we need to understand the new pipeline as something much more dynamic and complex. Capitalising on this reality will require institutions and industry partners to become more flexible and responsive in meeting the needs of learners.

Indeed, it would be beneficial to reconceptualise the supply and learning associated with developing STEM capability as a process of ongoing exchange. Teaching professionals, for example, would undoubtedly benefit from regular periods of industry experience to deepen and update their existing knowledge. Similarly, STEM industry professionals, once adequately equipped, would be able to dip into the teaching environment, perhaps at regular intervals, in ways that

---

[143] Butin 2003
[144] www.successfulstudents-stem.org.au/home

would also assist in building valuable networks and relationships while developing a base of educational practice.

For both streams, teachers and industry professionals, it may be useful to frame this within the current rubric of experiential or work-integrated learning. However, in addition to recognising secondments or professional placements, we need better ways of assessing and providing credit for the experience that industry professionals gain in their work. This could be supplemented by micro-training that would not require a PST to bear the time and financial cost of undertaking postgraduate studies, which currently act as a significant impediment.

More needs to, and can, be done to provide our new generations of lifelong learners with the foundations of learning and experience that will enable them to make these transitions in and out of teaching. One way, for example, may be to place greater emphasis on communication in undergraduate STEM degrees. The challenges will be to do this in a way that causes minimum disruption to current curriculum structures, which are already full of discipline content. One way around this would be to adapt small class teaching, so that students gain experience through structured team-based learning and other activities where students are required to demonstrate, explain and lead discussion. This was the approach taken by the *Communicating Science* activity.

A question remains, why are more STEM students at university not electing to enter teaching? This is, at least in part, a problem with the way the teaching profession is perceived. This is understandable when the experience of school is a negative one. But this experiential bias obscures how rewarding and stimulating teaching can be. In STEM teaching especially, teachers have real power to effect change through their own creative input. This is precisely what participants in ReMSTEP experienced where they collaborated with experts to design and deliver new activities. In this way, ReMSTEP has contributed to this re-imagining of the teaching practice. In addition, it is also possible that the widespread inclusion of work-integrated learning in undergraduate degrees will have a positive impact by exposing students to non-school work environments that have own challenging attributes as well. It is too early yet to know with certainty whether ReMSTEP has succeeded in increasing the supply of teachers as, for example, those participating in the MTeach degree will not graduate until 2018. However, the innovations have shown what elements might usefully be incorporated into a wider approach to the problem of supply.

Students enrolling in STEM degrees do so in order to work in industry or research. Overall, they do not embark on their degrees to become teachers. Numerous participants expressed these aspirations. While ReMSTEP was certainly successful in making some students positively disposed towards the idea of teaching at some point, one of the challenges lies in changing the way students understand the function of the degree. In short, we want students to understand from the outset that a degree based on mathematics and science is a pathway into teaching *in addition to* traditional STEM careers.

Part C

Findings and implications of the project

Introduction

Part A of this book laid out persistent, international concerns about mathematics and science education. We explored the nature and dimensions of the challenges inherent in improving teaching, student engagement, attainment and participation in mathematics and science in primary, lower secondary, upper secondary and tertiary education revealed by previous research.

Major imperatives identified through this research were examined, including aligning school mathematics and science with contemporary disciplinary practice and reforming PST education to incorporate these practices. Based on the research literature, of particular significance was the need to address the mindsets and identities of both students and teachers in these subject areas in order to break powerful, long-term, self-reinforcing cycles of traditional approaches to classroom practice. In other words, reconceptualisation at meta- and individual-levels was needed.

Part A also canvassed the background to Enhancing the Training of Mathematics and Science Teachers program (ETMST) arising from the above phenomena and concerns, and the five broad projects it comprised, one of which was *Reconceptualising Mathematics and Science Teacher Education Programs* (ReMSTEP). The logic, aims and features of ReMSTEP were outlined (See Appendix 3 p. 190).

Part B provided case studies drawn from the various activities carried out under ReMSTEP to address the seven intended innovations (with their original titles):

1. *Contemporary mathematics and science integrated in initial teacher education units of study*
2. *Undergraduate mathematics and science students engaging with schools*
3. *Mathematics and science teaching specialisations within initial teacher education primary programs*

Findings and implications of the project 151

4. *Specialist science and technology centre collaborations*

5. *Opportunities for students to interact with scientists in world-class research environments*

6. *Building on existing initial teacher education candidate expertise in mathematics and science*

7. *Building a recruitment pipeline of high-potential mathematics and science teachers*

Within Part C, Chapter 10 provides an overview of the outcomes and impacts of the various activities comprising ReMSTEP in total.

Chapter 11 then explores the broader implications of these findings along with issues such as sustainability, both of the ReMSTEP activities, and of changes to mathematics and science teacher education more generally as well as the teaching of these subjects in schools.

Chapter 10

Overall findings of ReMSTEP

Stephen Dinham, Russell Tytler, Deborah Corrigan, David Hoxley

Introduction

Appendix 1 (p. 188) provides a high-level overview of ReMSTEP achievements. As illustrated, ReMSTEP in total comprised:

- collaborations between 11 faculties across four universities, 10 external science partners and 24 primary and secondary schools

- 24 new education programs or program enhancements ('activities') that affected 2894 PSTs and undergraduate mathematics and science students over three years, and enabled interactions with over 200 scientists, mathematicians and academics.

As part of the latter stages of ReMSTEP an evaluation officer, Yuan Gao, not part of the actual activities comprising the project, was employed to gather extra evaluative and impact data across the various activities and innovations.

What follows is drawn both from evaluative data pulled from the individual activity teams and from the data gathered by Yuan Gao from project participants.

The project approach

The central focus of ReMSTEP was on introducing PSTs to contemporary mathematics and science to establish their conceptions of these subjects as discovery and application practices. In other words, a reconceptualisation from a traditional paradigm that mathematics and science knowledge is fixed and 'hard' and consists of solving problems using known techniques, towards a more realistic paradigm that mathematics and science are about discovering and applying new knowledge to solve real-world contemporary and future problems. The work of mathematicians and scientists is central to this problem solving.

ReMSTEP has introduced new approaches to mathematics and science teacher education that develop teachers' capabilities to represent these practices in their classrooms. Rather than implementing a singular and purpose-built course structure, this project created appropriate conditions for simultaneous developmental activity across diverse teacher education programs and sites of mathematical and scientific practice. A range of collaborative activities were initiated, including:

- introducing new courses, subjects and content into university teacher education programs

- establishing a variety of collaborative activities between university education, mathematics and science departments

- strengthening partnerships with external mathematics and science organisations

- creating a network of academics, pre-service and in-service teachers, teacher educators and scientists

- disseminating findings through a variety of mechanisms, including the ReMSTEP website[145], two ReMSTEP conferences in 2015 and 2016[146], a final report to the Commonwealth Government[147], this book and other forms of dissemination such as conference presentations and publications arising from the various activities comprising both ReMSTEP and the ETMST.

---

145   www.ReMSTEP.org.au
146   See http://remstep.org.au/conference/
147   Dinham 2017

Appendix 2 (p. 189) provides a network diagram detailing the novel connections between departments, institutions, primary and secondary schools and other important bodies, created by ReMSTEP activity.

Table 10.1 provides details of the numbers of tertiary students—both PST education, mathematics and science candidates—involved in the various ReMSTEP activities.

Table 10.1: Number of tertiary students involved in ReMSTEP activities

Activity	Number of tertiary students		
	2014	2015	2016
Advancing Science by Enhancing Learning in the Laboratory for schools (ASELL for Schools—Victorian node)		5	5
Australian Mathematics & Science Partnership Program (AMSPP)	82	84	53
Back to School (B2S)		30	18
Communicating Science/Institute for Frontier Materials (IFM)	298	332	315
Contemporary science school project		10	5
Contemporary science workshops			10
Creation of mathematics teaching videos (Mathematics videos)			17
Discovery Science and Technology Centre Bendigo (Discovery Centre)			185
Engaging in practices of contemporary sciences (EDF5674)		16	9
FARLabs	230	240	180

Gene Technology Access Centre (GTAC) partnership	5	24	
Growing Tall Poppies (GTP)	12	20	15
Inquiry Science	n/a	n/a	n/a
Institute of Frontier Materials (IFM) research practices video-supported activity modules	n/a	n/a	n/a
Multidisciplinary Science and Technology in Education (MSTE) program	10	15	17
Multimedia resources for biology and environmental education		105	85
New Science and Mathematics Elective		54	25
Quantum Victoria	n/a	n/a	n/a
Reconceptualising Chemistry	19	13	24
Reconceptualising Rocks		35	37
Schools Science Project (SCI3910) (SSP) and Monash Science Squad (MSS)		47	36
Science and mathematics specialist pathways in Masters of Teaching (Primary)	42	41	40
Science Students in Schools (SSIS)/ Science in Schools (SIS)		12	13
Scientists as Partners in Education (SPiEs)		5	7
Stem Cell Exploration	3	2	7
Total	701	1090	1103
		Total	2894

ReMSTEP impact

ReMSTEP has resulted in significant impacts on a number of organisations and people, which were evaluated by a combination of qualitative and quantitative approaches. The qualitative data was mainly gathered through interviews with key academics and scientists who ran the various ReMSTEP activities. The interview tool can be found in Appendix 4 (p. 191). Quantitative data was obtained through a variety of survey tools that were distributed either in person or via SurveyMonkey. An example of the survey tools used can be found in Appendix 5 (p. 194).

Overall, evaluative data has shown that ReMSTEP has been successful and fruitful in a variety of aspects, including:

- establishing a network of key agencies involved in science and science teacher education
- intensifying productive connections between university mathematics and science education academic staff
- making observable changes in PSTs' perceptions of and attitude towards scientists and science and/or mathematics teaching and learning
- improving the capacity of both PSTs and in-service teachers in integrating mathematics and contemporary science practice into curricula.

These broad outcomes are explored in more detail below.

Collaborations and networks

STEM researchers and agencies

Through the project, in-depth, extensive and hopefully sustainable collaborations and partnerships have been developed among different faculties of higher education institutions, science and technology research centres, local primary and secondary schools, and other public organisations (e.g. Melbourne Museum). This breadth and depth of collaborations has never been achieved between the partners before ReMSTEP. A reciprocal collaboration model has been created between the research agencies and higher education institutions. As another reliable and credible source of information and knowledge, research agencies offer valuable resources for universities, which they can access easily on-site and online. PSTs and undergraduate mathematics and science students were also rewarded by being involved in ReMSTEP, as it provided them with the opportunity to 'learn different educational practices, which inform improvements to their own training process'[148]. In addition, the PSTs and mathematics and science undergraduates who visited specialist centres such as Melbourne Museum have become enthusiastic ambassadors and advocates for these agencies. Hopefully they will transfer these experiences and this enthusiasm into their future classrooms and encourage their students to connect with these sites and resources, maintaining the collaboration in the long term.

Working with the PSTs and mathematics and science undergraduates were valuable educative experiences for research scientists to understand how university students learn, as there are not many opportunities for them to be involved in such teaching activities. It gave the scientists and mathematicians a new lens to see the discipline they are working in and allowed them to reconstruct the public image of research scientists and their work. As Dermot Henry (Deputy Director, Sciences, Museums Victoria) put it:

> Scientists are not necessarily boring people who spend all the time in a laboratory, but by and large are very fun-loving people. Geology is not only about the product, such as the rocks, but also about interesting process like the volcanism. I'm always keen to spread the world about geology through the community in lots of different ways.

---

[148] Luca Bertolacci, coordinator from VSSEC, MTeach program

Most importantly, through ReMSTEP, mathematicians and scientists have gained experience in presenting and communicating their work to a scientifically literate, but not expert, audience. High-level communication skills are an increasing priority for research departments for explaining their work and its importance to stakeholders, the public and potential future students. The scientists[149] do not always have the ability to translate their own research into everyday language to make it understandable. For many scientists, this experience made them more aware of what is involved in communicating to non-expert audiences, and they gained a better understanding of tailoring the delivery of their research findings to these different audiences. They felt that the broader aspects of their research methodology, their own motivation for their research, and how that research can be used to address different problems should be emphasised[150]. This experience also assisted research scientists to reflect on the ways that their research could be presented in the school curriculum. It helped them grow the capacity to adapt their research and their language to the school level and identify appropriate resources and tools to support the schools.

Visiting the research agencies, and interacting with the scientists there, has resulted in the PSTs and mathematics and science undergraduates re-examining their perceptions of the role of these agencies and of research scientists. According to the results of student (including both PSTs and mathematics and science undergraduates) surveys, the large majority of respondents across different activities agreed that they gained new insights into scientists' research and development practices and roles. Around half of the participants reported positive change in their perceptions of scientists as people. The majority of respondents who indicated no change in their perceptions explained that these had already been positive. The interviews carried out with the participants further illustrate how these changes happened. For example, touring the laboratories and storage units underneath and

---

149   Once again, 'scientists' can be taken to include mathematicians, unless otherwise specified.
150   Scientists' survey, *Reconceptualising Chemistry*

behind the Melbourne Museum provided students with an insight into the significant role that the Museum staff have in contemporary research.

> I didn't know there was so much research. Like when we went underneath ... I didn't realise all that was there. I didn't know any of that happened. I didn't even think about the fact they would do research ... and lots of the stuff that was actually on show—that they might use that for the research and stuff. (PST, *Reconceptualising Rocks*, 2016)

PSTs also realised the importance of the Melbourne Museum in information sharing and now regard it as a hub of education and resources. In addition, the experience of the scientists' presentations offered PSTs insights into the life of professional scientists and the realities of research:

> I did really enjoy it, it's not every day that I get to see a scientist speak about their work, and the method involved in the work. I didn't realise the exact process of how to go about finding things out ... it was really interesting to see the scientific method at work, by professionals. (PST, *Communicating Science*, 2015)

For some of the PSTs, this understanding of scientists and their work developed through the project reinforced their own identity as a teacher. It also enabled PSTs and in-service teachers to show their students the type of work they could aspire to, if they wanted to continue in a science pathway.

Cross-faculty collaboration

Another significant success of the ReMSTEP collaboration was the cross-faculty engagement in mathematics and science teacher education. Education and mathematics and science academics gained familiarity with each other's work and forged ongoing relationships, which significantly decreased the isolation between the two groups.

Academics from different faculties met on a regular basis to share insights, expert knowledge and resources across diverse activities. The science departments are now open to lending equipment to PSTs, and pathways have been opened that encourage teaching-related projects to be finished within some professional practice units; for instance, some science academic staff allow teaching students to produce lesson plans and resources as part of their assessment tasks.

Through the collaboration, education academics developed their communication skills with other academics and research staff and agencies. They became 'more aware of their facilitator or conduit role between the Faculty of Science academics and the PSTs, due to their expertise in working with children, and their knowledge of the limitations where the PSTs might go with science education'[151]. As science teacher educators, their own understanding of science education, and in particular science, technology, engineering and mathematics (STEM) education, has evolved through the interaction with science academics:

> I feel like that first year in particular it was the skills and understandings from each of the disciplines science, technology, engineering and mathematics was slightly lost. They were having lots of fun, but I think it became a bit difficult to really pin point those disciplines and develop those specific underpinning skills and ideas there. I feel like as we went through we learned that students really needed more, as we gave them the underpinning framework for science. What unites the STEM disciplines and why do we put them together. That made me think; well the framework that needs to underpin a STEM-based approach to education is a statistical framework. A framework that actually requires a student to think initially about a question that they can ask that has specific elements to it that can be answered through collecting numerical, quantitative data … which was for me a massive, huge light bulb moment. (Duncan Symons, MTeach lecturer in science education, UoM, 2016)

---

[151] Duncan Symons, MTeach lecturer in science education, UoM

Accompanying the cross-discipline collaboration are innovations in teaching approaches. As Dr Jo Raphael commented:

> It just helps me to view my pedagogy differently when I can mix it up with another area, so what was able to happen was that my science colleague was able to come into my drama education class, I was able to go into her science education class, and we were able to put our combined knowledge together to produce something new and different and interesting. So, it keeps my practice fresh and alive by being able to do that. (Dr Jo Raphael, art teacher–educator, *Stem Cell Exploration*, 2016)

The education academics appreciated the enormity and wealth of knowledge that was brought to the table by the academics from the Faculty of Science. As Duncan Symons put it:

> Because they have a breadth of understanding of science concepts, that actually they were not too focused on one specific area of science [was an advantage]. I think that probably if we were dealing with scientists who are very niche focused, for example, if they were in a medical laboratory and they were researching a very specific form of disease, then I think it would have been less valuable. (Duncan Symons, MTeach lecturer in science education, UoM, 2016)

For mathematics and science academics, the collaboration with Faculty of Education academics provided them an opportunity to reflect on their own teaching and learn about pedagogy in mathematics and science teaching.

> One of the problems with universities is that scientists lecturing in science do not have any education background so they have no idea of the pedagogy. It's a huge problem because the way they teach is the way they were taught, which typically is very didactic and not well thought through. They stood and essentially taught from

the textbook. And most of us turn around and do the same thing because it is very content laden in science courses to get through all this content with no appreciation that 80 per cent of it doesn't really get in. So, it is better to take this content and make the ideas really stick ... it requires teaching approaches to achieve that so they can go away and learn more about it, which is an education approach. (Science academic, 2016)

Working closely with each other also encouraged academics to reflect on the difficulties that they encountered throughout the engagement. The main barriers in cross-faculty collaboration include lack of discipline and education knowledge, and challenges related to commitment of time and energy. It became difficult when academic staff from mathematics and science and other disciplines, who do not necessarily have a background in education, attempted to cross that boundary. PSTs 'usually have very limited subject knowledge, so it was difficult for the academic staff to know where to begin and end'[152]. This is echoed by some science academics, as they commented that people who had been brought up in a science background entirely and taught in science probably do not know what it means to be involved in teacher education. These difficulties, although not universal across ReMSTEP activities, indicate that a cultural shift in the way education and science faculty staff interrelate may need nurturing and, at some point, would need to be recognised at a more formal level (such as workloads and for tenure/promotion) in respective faculties to enable sustainability.

Interaction with local schools

This project also encouraged the interaction between universities and local schools and resulted in better-prepared university academics who possess the willingness, enthusiasm and skills to engage with schoolteachers. In addition, dialogues have been set up between the schools that participated in this project to share experiences and classroom teaching

---

[152] Duncan Symons, MTeach lecturer in science education, UoM

practices, which was not a common occurrence before ReMSTEP. The schoolteachers reportedly gained much in terms of professional development, particularly in terms of science-based, enquiry-based learning, collaboration, effective teaching and contextualised experiences. As commented by one of the interviewed teachers:

> I have to say; we didn't have much experience of science at Teachers' College. So, for me this is a real reinvigoration of what I have learnt in the past. And I hope that I can build on it. I'd like to become more proficient and feel confident about my teaching about the concepts of science. In the past I have probably been the person who tries to engage the children. But to the best of my teaching I've probably been more the director and I've been the person who is out the front giving the information to the children. Whereas, this sort of experience lends itself to the children enquiring more. (Schoolteacher, *Schools Science Project & Science Squad*, 2016)

Practising teachers were keen to pursue more extensive collaboration outside the project. The experience with ReMSTEP also led to a change in teaching styles, as one of the interviewed teachers advised:

> The program encouraged me to change my teaching style, from focusing on the curriculum to getting the students interested; from focusing on the result to focusing on getting the students to go through the scientific process. Rather than concerning about whether the students learn the fact right or not, I have put in more efforts to bring the scientific thinking into the classroom and make the students think like a scientist. (Schoolteacher, *Reconceptualising Rocks*, 2016)

ReMSTEP activities also produced a variety of resources for schoolteachers to use, which feature contemporary science practices. For example, the *Stem Cell Exploration* activity offered valuable resources to teachers across Victoria, who can now implement a new aspect of the VCE study design in Unit Two and have resources and support to enable them to do so. The *Advancing Science by Enhancing Learning in the Laboratory* activity demonstrates the change that ReMSTEP had brought to the resources producing approach:

> Before the establishment of the partnership with ReMSTEP, the focus had been on laboratory activities that were scientifically sound and applied good pedagogy. However, the generation of student interest and relevance were not prominent. Since the formation of the partnership, the Victorian Node [of ASELL] has focused on the inclusion of contemporary science and industry links and the development of science conceptual learning. The involvement of ReMSTEP in ASELL Victoria has changed the priorities and sharpened the focus. There has been an attempt to integrate representational challenges into the laboratory activities although there is still work to be done in this area. This was not a goal before the partnership with ReMSTEP and is not evident in the approach of other nodes. (Focus group, ASELL for Schools in collaboration with ReMSTEP, 2016)

As ReMSTEP was focused on PSTs we did not investigate the primary and secondary school student experience with ReMSTEP activities, although ethics approval was obtained for other aspects of the project involving the adult participants. Rather, PSTs and in-service teachers observed and reported the impact of ReMSTEP on school students. According to the results of PSTs' and in-service teachers' surveys, respondents across different activities agreed their school students had developed new understanding of the nature of scientific practices as a result of the project. Almost all respondents observed that their students were productively engaged with learning mathematics and science. A majority of participants believed these activities, featuring contemporary scientific practices, had a positive effect on students' engagement with mathematics and science. Specifically, practising teachers noted that students who participated in the *Growing Tall Poppies* activity were more likely to participate in senior secondary science subjects, in particular physics, after participating in the project (AMSPP). They also commented on the interest of their students in the topic material was much higher than what would normally have been achieved in the classroom. In the *Discovery Science and Technology Centre* activity, the students were highly engaged and teachers expressed an intention to follow up with similar exploratory activities in their classrooms.

Impact on PSTs

The project provided new study options and extra experiences to infuse PSTs with cutting-edge mathematics and science practices. According to the responses of PST surveys, the majority reported a positive experience with different ReMSTEP activities. All surveyed PSTs reported that this had been a valuable part of their teacher education and professional development experience. Almost all respondents reported they enjoyed participating in this project and agreed that the process had been effective in supporting their learning and professional development. The majority of PSTs felt ReMSTEP works well. Participants also acknowledged the valuable opportunity that the project had provided them with to collaborate with research scientists on an authentic mathematics and science project.

New knowledge and skills

The most notable outcome that ReMSTEP achieved is a series of changes the project induced in PSTs' knowledge, skills, perceptions, attitude and capacity about mathematics; mathematics and science; and science teaching. Engaging with either the mathematics and science academic staff or the scientists in research centres or other public organisations provided the PSTs with up-to-date knowledge and practice in a variety of areas. The survey data showed that a range from half to all of respondents reported they had learnt some useful and interesting science concepts through the project.

Working side-by-side with research scientists provided PSTs with a more in-depth understanding of a science topic and current research in the area. They could view latest research facilities across different laboratory sites and gain insights into how current research is applicable to consumer and industrial applications. Some PSTs could better understand how some fundamental theories of science were applied in current research projects. They were also exposed to practical activities with an enquiry and contemporary science focus and engaged in reflection on what makes a good laboratory learning activity. In addition, PSTs learned different approaches to teaching mathematics and science, including the 5E model[153] and action research[154]. The latter, for example, shows how mathematics could be designed to be engaging rather than 'static':

> So when we were organised into tribes and being placed in primary school settings, my tribe decided to specifically focus on statistics. So what we did we created our own situation. So I said I wanted to buy a puppet for the class, but she doesn't know what puppet to get. So we read a picture book and the students had to identify which character appeared most to help me make a decision what puppet to buy. So we designed a picture graph together as a class and they were really engaged because they really wanted to know which puppet I would buy for my class next year. (PST, *Back to School*, 2016)

PSTs have also highlighted the value of bringing applied knowledge to the classroom:

> A lot of students have the 'why am I doing this?' and 'how can I use this knowledge in careers related to science?' The project enabled me to display my passion and to show my students how biology can go beyond the classroom. There is meaning to why we teach these difficult complex ideas. (PST, *Multimedia resources for biology and environmental education*, 2016)

---

153 5Es model: engage, explore, explain, elaborate and evaluate
154 See http://www.aral.com.au/resources/guide.html, for example

Shifted perceptions and attitude

The experience with ReMSTEP also led to a shift in PSTs' perceptions of and attitude towards science and science teaching. The survey data showed that a range from one-third to all PSTs across activities observed a positive change in their attitude towards mathematics and science teaching, and in their understanding of the role of mathematics and science teacher.

Experience with ReMSTEP allowed PSTs to develop new perspectives of a particular science area. To the PSTs, science was no longer seen as 'all-known' or contained within a textbook, but as a dynamically evolving process:

> I have noticed a change in that I now see that geology is an evolving science that has a role in the future of our earth and is not just a science of learning about the past. I can now see the importance of this science in our everyday lives and think it is important that students are made aware of this. (PST, *Reconceptualising Rocks*, 2015)

> I have thought a lot more about the disconnect between secondary science and real science. Without it [EDF5674] I probably would have still taught secondary science in a very traditional high school way. But I am very conscious now of why I shouldn't do that and why I should challenge the textbook sort-of ideas, because it is true that it doesn't reflect what really happens in [science] research. ... It has given me permission to change the way I teach it. (PST, *Engaging in practices of contemporary sciences*, 2016)

> I think one of the best aspects of the digi [explanation] is that it forces you to think about why you are teaching a topic/concept. It brings relevance to the curriculum both for the teachers and the students. Sometimes teaching science can feel like you are just regurgitating the curriculum. Producing a digi [explanation] brings perspective. (PST, *Multimedia resources for biology and environmental education*, 2016)

In some cases, previously unpleasant experiences of learning a science subject had been replaced by new positive perceptions of the same subject:

> I found earth science not as interesting as other science areas during my secondary school experience. However, this program allowed me to understand how interesting earth science can be when presented by passionate and knowledgeable individuals. (PST, *Reconceptualising Rocks*, 2015)

> It shows that mathematics relates to the real world around us. Makes it more interesting, rather than dry and boring. It helps us understand about applications of mathematics. Good to know where graphic designing and pixels of pictures come from—I did not know that there is mathematics behind these. (PST, *Mathematics videos*, 2016)

A PST who participated in the *Reconceptualising Chemistry* activity reminisced about his own high school experience, having found chemistry 'a very hard and confusing topic' and had questioned the importance of what was being taught in secondary schools: 'Why are we learning this, what's the point, am I ever going to use it in the future?' His perception changed through taking part in ReMSTEP, as he was presented with ways that scientists had applied their chemistry learning and understandings to research problems. Through ReMSTEP, he gained the insight that 'it was good to be able to see that, see many ideas, we got to see all the presentations not just the one we were working with, so having a whole lot of applications and being able to use it was really good'. The new perception of a particular science subject enables PSTs to link the subject with other areas of study. As one of the PSTs in *Reconceptualising Rocks* described, 'I think it sort of highlighted the connection between earth science and other areas, so, history, chemistry, biology and physics or the sort of big ones in the school curriculum'. Such understanding could contribute to implementing integrated STEM units of study in school at different levels.

In addition, the ReMSTEP activities offered PSTs a lens through which they could recognise the importance and value of integrating contemporary science into the classroom, particularly as there are not a lot of appropriate resources suited for the VCE resources cast in a language that is accessible to the students.

> I think there is a real lack of connection between the VCE expectations, around what is expected for people to understand, and then having that as something that is contemporary, and what we are currently doing in Australia, promoting science in Australia. (PST, *Multimedia resources for biology and environmental education*, 2016)

Others emphasised the importance of connecting with industry, particularly those who don't have an industry background:

> Industry experience versus classroom experience, bringing the two together and being able to pool resources is very valuable in the classroom ... finding reliable resources was challenging and working directly with scientists added significantly to the quality and credibility of the content. (PST, *Multimedia resources for biology and environmental education*, 2016)

A number of PSTs also highlighted the importance of linking mathematics and science learning to the real world:

> I do think it has changed my view on the purpose of [teaching] science. For me it's about providing students with all the tools so that they can go out into the world and when they see a whole lot of texts that are science-related they can come to their own conclusion on them. (PST, *Engaging in practices of contemporary sciences*, 2016)

> It will also assist the students to combine knowledge from the classroom and then take that outside into the real world to understand a particular issue. Having that on the school grounds and a forest nearby, for example, provided an opportunity for students to connect the classroom learning to outside the classroom learning. Rather

than just sticking with the notes, they engage at different levels. Even moving from the classroom to outside helps the students to refocus on a new aspect. (PST, *Back to School*, 2016)

The shifted perceptions of science also encouraged PSTs to redefine their role of science (and mathematics) teachers, being facilitators of learning rather than transmitters of content, as illustrated by the following statement:

Especially with science knowledge, I can be there to point out resources and do demonstrations but in this day and age of information, if you want to know about penguins then you can watch a David Attenborough documentary on YouTube. You have all your information at your fingertips. I can understand that back in the day you could just have an *Encyclopaedia Britannica* and a teacher and that's where you got your information. I see myself as someone that shows them the value, modelling what it might look like, but more as a facilitator. (PST, *Back to School*, 2016)

Moreover, the experience with ReMSTEP provided PSTs a chance to reflect on some issues existing in mathematics and science education at different levels. One is the use of information, communication and technology (ICT):

There are often advantages of integrating ICTs into the learning to provide students visualised learning experiences, and allow them to collaborate online. They can help to overcome some of the resistance points in students' learning because it is a natural aspect of their lives, reducing the cognitive load and the struggle for the students will make it much more enjoyable for them. However, teachers also need to pay attention to the downside of using technology, avoiding making the students feel like putting the materials into a black box of technology without appreciating what it means. (PST, *Back to School*, 2016)

Some of the ReMSTEP activities provided PSTs opportunities to experience teaching at both primary and secondary levels, which allowed them to learn the difference between the two levels of education. As one of the PSTs commented:

> Differences between primary and secondary teaching are vast. For the issue of behavioural management, I think that secondary school students are more sensitive in the way that you interact with them. In the primary school setting this is not necessarily the case. The kids forget quicker at the primary school level than in the case of secondary school. (PST, *Back to School*, 2016)

Even within the secondary years, differences in students' learning experience were observed by PSTs:

> In Year 7, students are very excited. They have lots of ideas, lots of preconceptions about what science is from primary school. I had a lot of girls saying this is so exciting, we're doing 'real' science. In Year 9, it becomes a bit more formulaic. It seems like they have become used to being told what's the right way to do something. They were more concerned with getting it right rather than exploring the science through the task. Then by Year 11 they are just concerned with the facts. (PST, *Back to School*, 2016)

In relation to teaching approaches, the change of PSTs' perceptions of science has led to the transition of their focus from content teaching to promoting different mindsets in the classroom. As one of the PSTs stressed, 'One of the things I can do to change that mindset is through real-life examples using concrete materials to make it more accessible for the students'[155]. Other foci that changed included ongoing formative assessment and timely feedback to students rather than pre-and post-assessment. Understanding the nature of science

---

[155] PST, *Reconceptualising Rocks*

resulted in a change of attitude towards mistakes:

> I would be engaging students more and giving them the confidence to try ... it's OK to make mistakes. There is an element of failure in [doing] science as well. Scientist's ... big names still have that in [their work] ... as well. It's OK to fail. (PST, *Engaging in practices of contemporary sciences*, 2016)

Improved confidence and capacity

The knowledge and skills that PSTs gained from ReMSTEP together with their developed understanding of science and mathematics contributed to the improvement of their confidence in and capacity of teaching these subjects. According to the survey results, a range from one-third to all of the participants across different activities appreciated the engagement with new and interesting approaches to teaching mathematics and science and gained ideas for bringing contemporary mathematics and science practices into the school curriculum. The majority of PSTs agreed that they had gained valuable ideas about how to support students to learn what mathematics and science professionals do and the way they think. Almost all respondents felt they were more capable in understanding and communicating mathematics and science ideas to students. More than two-thirds of PSTs felt more confident in teaching mathematics and science-related topics at school.

Being exposed to cutting-edge science research has led to the growing confidence of PSTs in teaching science in their own practice:

> I have to say I am pretty OK with immunology and immunotherapy now. I would be pretty comfortable teaching it.' (PST, *Multimedia resources for biology and environmental education*, 2016)

> This program revealed that earth sciences can be much more engaging and relevant than I ever imagined. I feel much more prepared

and excited about approaching earth science in my teaching. (PST, *Reconceptualising Rocks*, 2016)

Constructing a coherent contemporary view of the nature of science and mathematics also provided PSTs with the language and confidence to engage in professional discourse, which challenged and further enriched their understandings of sciences. PSTs self-reported improved confidence and competence in their professional practice when exploring science with their students as a way of knowing and understanding the world.

The project also developed PSTs' capabilities of providing quality science teaching in five ways.

First, PSTs have honed their skills in applying enquiry-based learning. The examples given below illustrate this point:

> At the start, with the Biology 1 and 2 subjects we gave them a bag of yeast and we said prove to me how this is alive. That was for the first unit. Half the kids really took the bull by its horns and just did it. They came up with really inventive ways of proving it. I realised that it is good to incorporate more enquiry-based learning into my classroom. You need to get them to the level to engage in that enquiry or design their own experiments. I felt that was a lot more engaging for them. It took them a bit more time, but it was better than us putting a plant in water and letting a fan go and waiting to see how long the water level goes down. (PST, *Back to School*, 2016)

> I liked the 'story-telling' element of how a single rock/pebble has travelled through the rock cycle over millions of years. The use of a concept map helped, and I can see myself doing that with my students. Incorporating media/video presentations is something I would definitely like to do. (PST, *Reconceptualising Rocks*, 2016)

> We used the 'thinking through the lesson plan' template, which I found very useful. It focused on both the teacher and student learning.

> One of the best aspects of the template is that the lesson planning had things like 'what are your mathematical goals for the lesson?' or 'how would you anticipate student responses', or 'what are your expectations for students in what they are working on and for completing the task?' Those sorts of things provided one resource that accessed the important low-inference observation skills. So I think it was important for my professional development as a teacher. (PST, *Reconceptualising Rocks*, 2016)

Second, the PSTs found that they would be able to replicate experiments, if they did not need specialist or dangerous equipment or materials such as liquid nitrogen. They were able to produce their own lesson plan for their science topic, with ideas on how to teach that they would not have thought of or known about without ReMSTEP.

Third, PSTs were able to provide context to the principles that they will teach to their students when they enter the classroom. By engaging with a scientist and 'trying to get them to talk about the overall picture of the applications' (PST, *Reconceptualising Chemistry*), PSTs could justify the pedagogical value of teaching techniques and compare current research to the curriculum, a process which was reported by the participants as thought-provoking and valuable. PSTs indicated that the activities and lessons they developed through ReMSTEP would enable their future students to understand what a 'real' scientist was doing, the topics being explored and the current research.

Fourth, the ReMSTEP experience encouraged PSTs to implement integrated STEM teaching:

> Because of the STEM Australia initiative, the government wants every student to appreciate each of these four domains, but also integrate them more into each other. It is not like it will mesh into one big subject but more about interdisciplinary and integration of subjects. I would like to take a themed approach, like an aquarium for example, bring in physics such as the fluid dynamic of the fish swimming and

also the biodiversity. This would bring in all four subjects into one theme.' (PST, *Back to School*, 2016)

Fifth and finally, other techniques that PSTs learned through ReMSTEP include the 5E model used in their placement, the ongoing professional learning, peer coaching, low-inference observations and the integration of technology into science teaching, particularly since technology is now a common part of students' lives.

The benefits that PSTs have gained though ReMSTEP have the potential to be transformed into school contexts. The rewarding visits to the Melbourne Museum, the exciting excursions, or the process of working with scientists to develop teaching resources are all likely to be translated into primary or secondary schools and ultimately impact on students and their learning.

> The project was increasing the self-efficacy of these PSTs and changing their personal–professional identity in some aspects. They see themselves proficient in science and mathematics, hopefully both, and what we know is that if the teachers are going out and feeling confident, they would incorporate science on a regular basis, into their work programs, make it enjoyable and give students that appetite for learning science, then it should flow through to the ultimate purpose, which is to increase the students' learning outcomes. So if the most effective element that has the biggest impact on learning is a quality teacher, if we are producing more high-quality mathematics and science teachers then it follows that we are going to increase student learning outcomes. (Dr Melody Anderson, MTeach (Primary) coordinator, UoM, 2016)

Impact on tertiary mathematics and science students

Another key aspect of the ReMSTEP project was to offer an opportunity for university mathematics and science (non-PST) students to engage with schools in order to build a 'recruitment pipeline' of high-potential mathematics and science teachers. The mathematics and science undergraduate, and higher-degree research students have learned the complexities and challenges of the teaching landscape, and increased their capabilities by engaging with students, PSTs and scientists. This has increased their ability to teach and explain the mathematics and science that they are learning or researching. Some of the mathematics and science students noted that they would be continuing their work into a scientific field, while others were motivated to consider taking up one of the available pathways to teaching as a career.

According to interviews with science students, ReMSTEP helped them develop a new understanding of science teaching and learning, including teaching as a complex activity, different teaching approaches and the use of technology to enable teaching. They learned that many different components fit together in teaching, such as classroom management, content and pedagogy.

The innovative and effective use of ICT in classes that mathematics and science students attended resulted in changing attitudes towards the role of ICT in teaching. Rather than ICT being seen as distractors for students, when employed in an appropriate way it was acknowledged that ICT can engage students and improve learning. Rather than 'feeding' the students with information, using ICT enables learner-centred teaching, which focuses on discovering information. In this case, students 'feed' themselves, as shown in the example below:

> At high school one of the tasks they have to do is introduce 3D shapes to their friends and they have to teach each other about these shapes. So for the 3D shapes lesson, the teacher divided instruction into three sections, such as easy level, intermediate level and advanced level. What I learned from this was that they have to plan their lessons around these different categories, so they have these 3D models and the students need to interact with them in specific ways. One of the ways they did this was to find a model they were working on online, say a pyramid. So they can find out how to identify the pyramid and then relate this to the physical model they have in the classroom. Then they can show it to people and explain it. (Science undergraduate, *Back to School*, 2016)

Participating in ReMSTEP also allowed university mathematics and science students to learn about the factors that impact student learning, and the experience helped them to understand that mathematics and science education needs to be tailored to the learner and that teachers of these subjects need to encourage questions and reflections rather than just lecturing about a topic. It thus highlighted the importance of making learning about mathematics and science interactive and engaging. A balance between the science content and the enjoyment of learning could be achieved. The experiences provided by ReMSTEP could also be transferred to their future work. As of one of the interviewees stated:

> After taking this course I felt more like a clinical interventional practitioner, which means I can clinically address or identify my students' weaknesses or areas they could work on and I could intervene by using different teaching approaches or switching methods to get them back on track. So from that aspect it does lead me to have higher employability. (Science undergraduate, *Science in Schools*, 2016)

More importantly, the experience with ReMSTEP made science students reflect on the value of teaching as a career and encouraged a number of them to consider taking up one of the available pathways to teaching as a career.

> I was thinking you never get told, 'oh you would be a great teacher'. You get told you be a great this, that and the other, scientist, musician, lawyers, never you would be a great teacher. (Science undergraduate, *Schools Science Project*, 2016)

> When I got into the ReMSTEP program I could see that there are not so many people who want to do teaching in mathematics. So it opened up a new perspective for me. I think teaching plays a very important part in young people's lives. And I think one of the ways that teaching feeds back into the community is education. (Science undergraduate, *Back to School*, 2016)

Some mathematics and science undergraduate students initially fostered ideas of becoming secondary teachers but changed their focus to possible careers in primary education:

> But now it is something I would consider—actually going into teaching. Personally I thought it wouldn't be as much primary school teaching, just because generally the teachers do not specialise as much in just one field as they do in high school teaching. Yeah, but now I would actually consider teaching a younger group than before. (Science undergraduate, *Schools Science Project*, 2016)

Pursuing a teaching career does not necessarily have to be in a school setting; it could be outside the classroom:

> My placement at GTAC offered me a valuable opportunity to teach outside the schools, which I found was very creative and exciting. And I plan to teach either in the school or in a science program such as through Melbourne Zoo or Museum Victoria. (Science undergraduate, *Science in Schools*, 2016)

Thus, through taking part in ReMSTEP, students on a career trajectory to become scientists and mathematicians gained an understanding and appreciation of the practice of teaching. This understanding will enhance their skills and abilities to communicate their research discoveries to the public and to younger age groups in particular, which will prove useful in their future careers.

> You have to get yourself down to the students' level, sitting down and talking to them, in order to see and feel the difference in taking that approach. (Science undergraduate, *Back to School*, 2016)

Chapter 11

Conclusions and implications

Russell Tytler, Deborah Corrigan

It is important to remember the parameters under which ReMSTEP was developed: four universities, working across faculties with specialist STEM centres to reconceptualise mathematics and science teachers' preparation. There are important lessons to be learnt, which we have outlined below.

The role of collaboration

The evaluative data show that cross-faculty engagement in science teacher education has been identified as one of the strongest outcomes of ReMSTEP. University mathematics and science departments and faculties, and mathematics and science education academic staff have established strong networks. Academics from different faculties met regularly to share and build expert knowledge, collaborate and develop resources across the diverse activities. Ongoing collaborative arrangements have been established in planning and maintaining teacher education courses and activities as well as educative activities in mathematics and science courses. At some point, this outcome would need to be formalised in the respective faculties to ensure sustainability, but ReMSTEP has demonstrated the possibility of a cultural shift in cross-disciplinary relations that can yield worthwhile outcomes for all. Such cultural shifts have relied on the respect for the expert knowledge and capabilities these different groups bring to these new collaborations. New subjects and pathways that have been introduced are, by their nature, likely to be more permanent than collaborations and partnerships that need maintenance. In these latter cases, time will tell if relationships and models of interaction pioneered under ReMSTEP become enduring features of practice.

Collaboration across universities was also an achievement in this project, although the instances of such collaborations are less extensive than those internal to universities. Similarly, while worthwhile collaborations were developed with specialist centres, the sheer effort in maintaining such collaborations makes them less sustainable. We need to consider how to create conditions that allow collaborative ventures greater opportunities for success and sustainability.

STEM and STEM education

ReMSTEP embodies the increasing recognition in Australia that the education of school students and citizens in STEM knowledge and skills, and appreciation of the STEM disciplines as important and worthwhile perspectives on the world, is the *joint* responsibility of the science and education communities. For instance, the Office of the Chief Scientist has pulled together an impressive listing of partnerships between the professional STEM community and the schooling system[156] reflecting growing interest on both sides of the R&D and education divide to explore the potential of these interactions. The Commonwealth Scientific and Industrial Research Organisation's (CSIRO) Scientists and Mathematicians in Schools program (SMiS) is an example of such interactions, with a high profile and national reach. Studies of the benefits for schools and the STEM R&D community are scarce, but those that do exist have shown benefits for all partners[157], including more engaging pedagogies; increased student knowledge, skills and attitudes; and outcomes for STEM professionals that include satisfaction with engagement with students, skills in communication and reflection on the purposes of their own work.

ReMSTEP has pioneered these interactions within the teacher education sphere, aiming to generate similar, if not even greater,

---

156 www.starportal.edu.au
157 Tytler et al. 2011

gains in the understanding of mathematics and science by PSTs and other STEM students, through partnerships with the STEM R&D and professional community. Chapter 10 has demonstrated positive outcomes, overall, for all participants: undergraduate mathematics and science students, PSTs, STEM education academics and scientists including science academics. The findings also attest to a suite of outcomes that we know are important for changing perceptions of mathematics and science, and the teaching within the STEM landscape. These include not only deepened knowledge, but also enhanced perceptions of the nature of STEM as a way of thinking and acting, the role of STEM practices, the potential for engagement with ideas and appreciation of the human nature of the STEM enterprise. It is these changes, towards a closer and more authentic relationship between school science and mathematics, and STEM R&D and professional practices, including a realisation of the concerns, enthusiasms and commitments of STEM practitioners that underpin the 'reconceptualisation' in the ReMSTEP title.

An important change agent in this process is that of the STEM education academic, who can act as a 'broker' between the highly stylised school mathematics and science and the STEM R&D practitioners and professionals. Without this brokering role, the opportunity for change is limited as the reconceptualisation aspects require rethinking on how contemporary mathematics and science and STEM practices can more broadly be engaged with in school settings. The role of the change agent is to challenge status quo thinking such as 'this is how I learnt mathematics and science and it worked for me'. They need to foster thinking that asks how schools can engage with the opportunities presented in contemporary mathematics and science and STEM ways of thinking and acting. Such thinking requires the development of new pedagogical approaches to realise such engagement, and the STEM education academic is a crucial change agent in this process. Additionally, the interactions between STEM education academics and STEM R&D practitioners and professionals has meant that for the education academics, the vista of possibilities has broadened considerably given the generosity of the collaborative efforts between these two expert groups. Evidence of such change is highlighted below.

A major achievement of ReMSTEP was to assist PSTs to change their stereotypes of mathematics and science teaching and develop their capacities to integrate contemporary mathematics and science into the school curriculum. Being exposed to cutting-edge mathematics and science research and practice allowed PSTs to develop new perspectives on the contemporary practice of mathematics and science, growing confidence in teaching difficult concepts, and updating their subject knowledge. *Innovation 1—Contemporary mathematics and science integrated into PST units of study* showed evidence of shifts in students' perceptions of the nature of science and its communication. There is evidence also that these rewarding experiences can be transformed into school contexts and ultimately benefit school students. While ReMSTEP focused on PST education, many of the activities focused on the development of school curricula and, in some cases, these were trialled in schools with positive outcomes for both students and teachers.

Part of the innovative work in representing contemporary STEM practice involved interactions with interdisciplinary research, such as with the Institute of Frontier Materials (IFM) that incorporates science and engineering, mathematics and digital technologies research. Further, many of the research stories encountered by PSTs involved significant societal issues, such as energy conservation, emissions minimisation, ethical issues shaping stem cell research or integrative ecology. Students encountered scientists' stories about day-to-day practice, commitments and value positions. They were exposed to methodologies such as simulations and modelling, industrial processes and economic constraints on practice. All these provided a much richer and more personal story about STEM practice than is normally encountered in traditional classrooms, and the evidence indicates that exposure to these stories has significant impact on PSTs' perceptions and potentially their future practice.

Ultimately, the underpinning rationale of ReMSTEP, in its introduction into teacher education, experiences of contemporary STEM practice, and of STEM practitioners, only makes sense in the context of a belief that these interactions and approaches can lead to a reinvigoration of school STEM teaching and learning. The PSTs that have experienced ReMSTEP activities may provide the seeding needed to introduce more engaging and challenging approaches into schools. This is by no means an easy ask, but we are encouraged in this hope by the observation that such activities, involving partnerships between schools and the STEM professional community, are increasingly common. We hope that beginning teachers with experience of ReMSTEP will be well positioned to be in the vanguard of this movement.

Allied with this focus on representing contemporary STEM practice in teacher education activity, ReMSTEP offered an opportunity for undergraduate mathematics and science students to engage with schools in order to build a recruitment pipeline of high-potential mathematics and science teachers. As a result of the activities that focused on this cohort of tertiary students, undergraduate mathematics and science students were motivated to consider taking up one of the available pathways to teaching as a career. There was also evidence that part of this motivation was the realisation for these students that teaching was a more deliberative and complex, and therefore worthwhile, undertaking than they had hitherto realised.

Finally, in terms of the STEM R&D community involved in interactions with education and with PSTs, there was evidence of positive outcomes also. For PhD students paired with PSTs to support the production of school activities translating their research, the experience gave them experience in communicating the social and technological relevance of their research, recasting their knowledge for a broader public. For senior science researchers also, the experience was generally positive, reflecting a commitment to working with PSTs in an education context to better promote STEM working and thinking, but to reconsider their own communication practices to those outside their professional peer group.

Implications and recommendations

ReMSTEP has innovated across a range of activities and institutions. It has demonstrated the viability and payoffs of collaborative arrangements between education and STEM faculties, to their mutual benefit. However, despite the size of the project and perhaps because of its complexity, much remains to be done to cement these innovations and findings into ongoing practice. While some of the activities are now cemented in course structures, many will continue to exist because of the relationships established and recognition of mutual benefit. Over time, these need to transform into established cultural practice. The relationships themselves, while positive, nevertheless contained some inevitable complexities and tensions in crossing boundaries between education and science, for instance. While partnerships between specialist centres and universities were very productive, this was not always the case, and ways must be found, in the absence of funding, to take what was learnt and embed it in ongoing partnership work.

While links between ReMSTEP and schools, where they existed, yielded positive outcomes, there were no formal evaluations of this work, given the ReMSTEP focus, and in many cases the translation of contemporary STEM capabilities into school activities led to resources which have yet to be tested in schools. There is a need to further investigate and refine the approaches to representing contemporary STEM practice into school practice, as well as into ongoing models of teacher education practice. Further to these investigations, there is a subsequent need to focus on the scalability of such approaches. Much still remains to be done.

There is thus much to be learnt from ReMSTEP, in terms of productive ways forward for mathematics and science teacher education, and in terms of potential extension of these ideas into the school curriculum. What follows is a set of implications, and recommendations, for ongoing research and practice that builds on what we now know from evidence gathered in the course of the project. ReMSTEP is one of a number of projects under the ETMST banner that linked STEM practitioners with educators. There is a need to carry forward what has

Conclusions and implications 185

been learnt, to inform the reforms to mathematics and science teacher education, and in STEM education more generally, across the system.

1. *Establishing sustainable practices involving collaboration between education and the sciences.* ReMSTEP has shown the possibilities and payoffs, and also some of the challenges, in partnerships between STEM and education faculties and individuals, and with specialist STEM education resource centres. These partnerships underpin the great variety of activities in ReMSTEP. There is a need to more precisely articulate the nature and rewards of such partnerships across the ETMST projects, together with processes involved in setting them up. Further, there needs to be additional research into the conditions under which ephemeral partnerships established during ReMSTEP can become established in formal university structures.

2. *Continuing, refining and expanding the models for incorporating contemporary STEM practice into PST education.* A range of models have been developed under ReMSTEP through which STEM R&D practitioners interact with PSTs, or with STEM education academics as their knowledge and practice is translated into teacher education and school activities. These models need to be further explored and developed as part of a longer-term strategy of engaging PSTs, teachers and education academics in deeper levels of STEM working and thinking, and in enhancing their appreciation of the nature of contemporary mathematics and science R&D practice.

3. *Recognising and formalising relations between universities and external education institutions.* A number of activities involved partnerships between the universities and specialist centres such as the Melbourne Museum, Gene Technology Access Centre or Quantum Victoria. These were generally very successful, once issues of timetabling and perspective had been ironed out. To varying extents, these activities depended on ReMSTEP

seeding funds. There is a need to explore ways of continuing this collaborative work through formalised arrangements that are mutually beneficial.

4. *Investigating ways of translating and extending these innovations into school STEM practice.* Many of the ReMSTEP activities involved developing school activities and partnerships with practising teachers. The rationale for this was clear—that STEM education academics led and scaffolded engagement of PSTs in thinking about their future practice through interactions with contemporary STEM R&D practitioners implied a need to translate these insights into school science activities. However, the wider agenda, beyond ReMSTEP, must be the representation of contemporary STEM practice in school curricula, as a means of engaging students more deeply with STEM ideas, ways of working and the people involved. There is a need to further explore the ReMSTEP innovations for their implications for school mathematics and science. This will involve working with teacher education and reform more broadly, which also includes working with the current STEM teacher workforce in Australian schools. There are significant funding implications of such work, but the findings of ReMSTEP and other ETMST projects demonstrate this may be a significant step forward.

5. *Investigating means of scaling up the ReMSTEP innovations.* ReMSTEP, and the ETMST initiatives more broadly, represent a taste for reform of mathematics and science teacher education based on interactions with contemporary STEM practice. There is a need to take what has been learned and investigate how to communicate this learning in ways that support applying these ideas to the higher education sector more generally.

6. *Tracking the outcomes of the project longitudinally, incorporating an ongoing research element.* ReMSTEP has pioneered a significant start to the exploration of STEM education partnerships in higher education, but because of the limited scope and timescale,

these achievements must be seen as a beginning. PSTs participating in ReMSTEP activities attest to changes in their views and potentially their future practice. It would be interesting and useful to track some of these teachers as they begin their professional lives, to test if the changes in perspective carry over into practice, and influence in schools. It would also be valuable to trace the influence of ReMSTEP on ongoing activity in the four universities.

7. *Undertake research to establish the conditions under which STEM R&D practices can be captured for PSTs, and teachers and students, to engender critical and creative reasoning.* We have explored a range of models of interaction between contemporary STEM R&D practitioners and educators, PSTs and teachers. Beyond this, there is a need for ongoing research that can identify the conditions of interaction, knowledge and capability transfer, that are important to change teacher perceptions about STEM practice, and about teaching and learning approaches that engage students more deeply.

ReMSTEP has pioneered a range of innovative approaches to mathematics and science teacher education that involve partnerships between educators and the STEM research and development community. Much has been achieved, yet much remains to be done. The project has provided evidence of the value of interactions between educators, students and the STEM research community. It has provided a 'proof of concept' of what could be a productive new direction for school STEM practice and for STEM teacher reform.

Appendices

Appendix 1: Overview of ReMSTEP achievements

Reconceptualising Mathematics and
Science Teacher Education Programs

remstep.org.au

Australian Government
Department of Education and Training

Supported by the Australian Government
Department of Education and Training

ReMSTEP formed collaborative partnerships
between 11 faculties
across 4 universities, who
collaborated with 10 external science partners
and 24 primary and secondary schools

These took the form of 24 new education programs or enhancements
that impacted 2879 pre-service teachers and graduate mathematics and
2894 ice students over 3 years
and
enabled interactions with over 200 scientists, mathematicians and academics

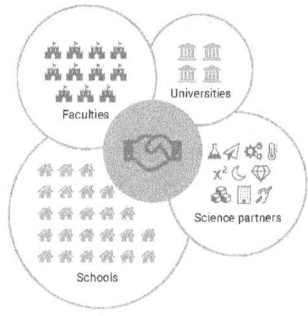

ReMSTEP has contributed to the goals of the Enhancing the Training of
Mathematics and Science Teachers Program through:

New study options developed in collaboration with science and mathematics departments and researchers
- delivering a cohort of graduate teachers better equipped to integrate mathematical and science practice into their classroom pedagogy.

Additional Experiences for pre-service teachers designed and delivered in collaboration with specialist centres
- providing opportunities for pre-service teachers to enrich their content knowledge and develop learning resources alongside practising scientists and mathematicians.

Units of study for Science and Mathematics students
- workplace experience giving high calibre science and maths students exposure to teaching as a career

Exemplars and resources
- resources, collaboration models and innovative pedagogies developed through the ReMSTEP activities will be shared with the education community.

Core to all ReMSTEP activity is collaboration across faculties, universities
and specialist science and maths centres, and the exploration of ways of
linking pre-service teachers to practising scientists and mathematicians,
in order to represent the creativity and drive of scientific and mathematical
thinking for these future teachers.

THE ReMSTEP PARTNERS

LA TROBE UNIVERSITY

MONASH University

THE UNIVERSITY OF MELBOURNE

Change the **MINDSETS** and **THINKING** of both students and teachers

Source: ReMSTEP 2018

Appendix 2: ReMSTEP connections

This network diagram details the novel connections between departments, institutions, primary and secondary schools and other important bodies, which ReMSTEP activity created.

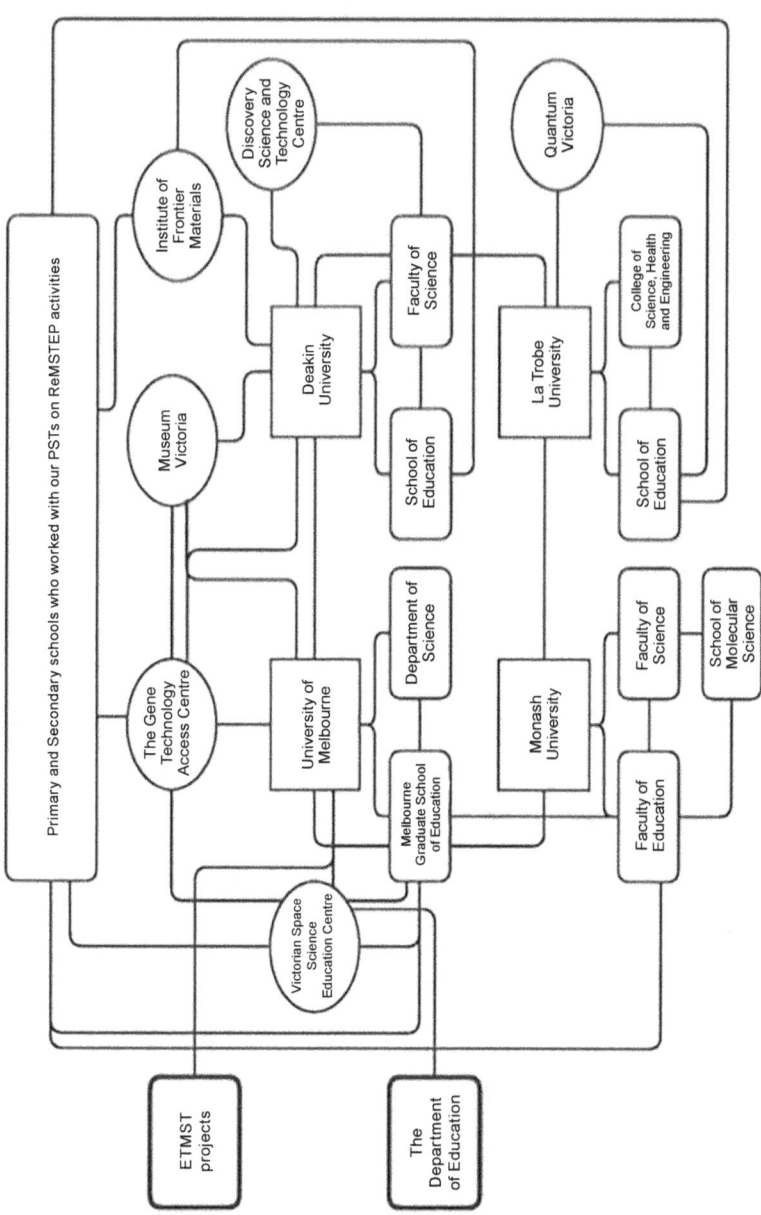

Source: ReMSTEP 2018

190

Appendix 3: The ReMSTEP Program logic

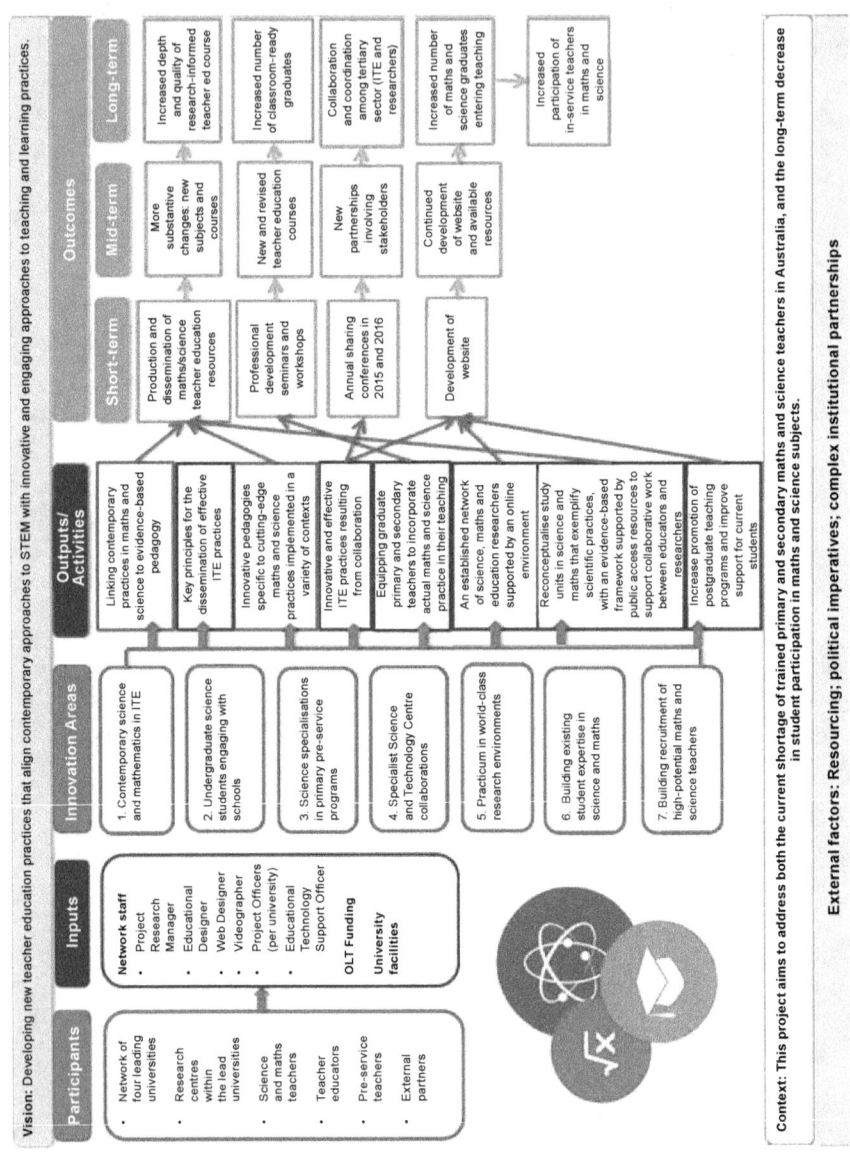

Source: ReMSTEP 2018

Appendix 4: Interview questions used during evaluation

Project overview

Project name

- Who was involved?
- What was done (in broad terms)?

Project rationale: What is the intention?

- Is there a theoretical basis or model, or literature that informed the project?
- What gaps do you see are addressed with this project?

Project activities

- What was the nature of the activities—provide examples?
- What was the nature of engagement of PSTs or teachers with contemporary mathematics/science practices?
- What aspects of mathematics/science practice were represented to the PSTs? How was this orchestrated? In what sense do you regard this as innovative or significant?
- What changed curriculum/classroom practices are envisaged, flowing from the project? By what means were these changes supported?
- What opportunities were there for mathematics/science students (undergrad or HDR) to reconceptualise their perceptions of school science or mathematics learning and teaching?

Results

Experience of participants

- What was the experience of PSTs or science and mathematics students, school students, teachers, scientists, teacher educators?

- What evidence is available to identify the experience? (surveys, notes, video, etc.)

Project outputs

- What resources were produced and what is their quality (and where can they be found)?

- What understandings or models have resulted, concerning how to engage PSTs with contemporary science and mathematics practice?

Project outcomes: What were the outcomes for the different players?

- Is there evidence of a cultural shift in the way education and science faculty staff interrelate as a result of this project?

- What have research scientists or mathematicians gained by participating in the ReMSTEP project? Have their views about teaching and learning science and mathematics changed as a result of the project?

- What have science or mathematics undergraduate or HDR students gained by participating in the project? Is there evidence of a shift in science or mathematics students' perception of teaching as a worthwhile career path?

- What evidence is there of improved learning and engagement of PSTs, or of teachers, as a result of the project? What did PSTs learn about the nature of science, or how to incorporate mathematics/science practices into the curriculum?

- What has been learnt about the efficacy of incorporating contemporary mathematics/science practices in the school curriculum? What evidence is there of improved learning and engagement of school students, as a result of the project?
- What principles can be taken from the project concerning processes for bringing contemporary science and mathematics research and development practices into teacher education?

Concluding discussion

Challenges

- What was the nature of challenges to successful implementation?
- What changes were made, from which we can learn?

Impact

- What is the short-/medium-term impact of the project (ongoing processes, commitments, existence of resources, over a 1–3 year projection)?
- What are the longer-term implications?

Sustainability

- What has been learnt about processes for incorporating contemporary science and mathematics practices in teacher education?
- In what sense is the project sustainable?

Scalability

- What is the possibility of the project processes and outcomes being reproduced at scale?

Appendix 5: Sample survey questions used during evaluation

The following questions were either asked in person or via SurveyMonkey. The response options were: Strongly agree / somewhat agree / neither agree nor disagree / somewhat disagree / strongly disagree / N/A. There was also an open-text box for additional comments. The questions given were:

As a result of the ReMSTEP activity:

1. I learnt some useful and interesting science concepts.
2. There has been a positive change in my attitude towards science and/or teaching science.
3. There has been a change in my understanding of the role of science teachers.
4. I have been surprised by what I learnt about mathematics/science practices, and how these might be represented in the curriculum.
5. I was engaged in new and interesting approaches to teaching science.
6. I have learnt things about engaging with contemporary science that will influence my teaching in the future.
7. I gained ideas for how to bring contemporary science practices into the curriculum.
8. I have gained experience in understanding and communicating mathematics/science ideas to students.
9. I gained valuable ideas about how to support students to learn about what mathematics/science professionals do, and their thinking.
10. I feel more confident in teaching mathematics/science-related subjects at school.

11. Students developed new understandings of the nature of scientific practices.

12. Students were productively engaged with learning science.

13. These activities featuring contemporary scientific practices positively impact on students' engagement with science.

14. I felt the ReMSTEP activity worked well.

15. I enjoyed the process of participating in this project.

16. The process was effective in supporting my learning/professional development.

17. I gained a lot by interacting with mathematics/science professional(s) in the project.

18. This has been a valuable part of my teacher education experience.

19. Other than the Science and Mathematics Specialisation Pathways in MTeach, have you participated in any other ReMSTEP activities?

20. Would you like to participate in an interview to further share your experience with ReMSTEP activities?

References

Aalderen-Smeets, S. I., & Walma van der Molen, J. H. (2015). 'Improving primary teachers' attitudes toward science by attitude-focused professional development'. *Journal of research in science teaching*, 52(5), pp. 710–34.

Adamuti-Trache, M., & Andres, L. (2007). 'Embarking on and persisting in scientific fields of study: Cultural capital, gender, and curriculum along the science pipeline'. *International Journal of Science Education*, 30(12), pp. 1–28.

Advancing Science by Enhancing Learning in the Laboratory (ASELL Schools) (n.d.). Retrieved 19 August 2017 from www.asell.org/Schools/About-ASELL.

Aikenhead, G. (2001). 'Students' ease in crossing cultural borders into school science'. *Science Education*, 85(2), pp. 180–88.

Aikenhead, G. (2006). *Science education for everyday life: Evidence-based practice*. New York: Teachers College Press.

Aikenhead, G. (2013). 'Science, Technology, Engineering and Mathematics Education and Related Employment for Indigenous Students and Citizens of Saskatchewan'. Contributing report to Marginson, S., Tytler, R., Freeman, B., & Roberts, K. (2013). *STEM: Country comparisons*. Melbourne: The Australian Council of Learned Academies. https://acola.org.au/wp/?s=STEM%3A+Country+comparison.

Ainsworth, S., Prain, V., & Tytler, R. (2011). 'Drawing to learn in science', *Science*, 333(26), pp. 1096–97.

Angus, M., Olney, H., Ainley, J., Caldwell, B., Burke, G., Selleck, R., & Spinks, J. (2004). *The sufficiency of resources for Australian primary schools*. Canberra: Australian Government Department of Education, Science and Training.

Archer, L., Hollingworth, S., & Halsall, A. (2007). '"University's not for me — I'm a Nike person": Urban, working-class engagement young people's negotiations of 'style', identity and education'. *Sociology*, 41(2), pp. 219–37.Australian Government. (nd).

Enhancing the Training of Mathematics and Science Teachers Program. Australian Government: Office for Learning & Teaching. (np) Available at: https://www.education.gov.au/enhancing-training-mathematics-and-science-teachers-program.

Australian Government. (2013). *Enhancing the Training of Mathematics and Science Teachers Program.* Australian Government: Office for Learning & Teaching. pp. 1–2.

Australian Government. (2016). *National innovation and science agenda.* www.innovation.gov.au/page/national-innovation-and-science-agenda-report.

Australian Maths and Science Partnerships Program (AMSPP), Department of Education and Training, Australian Government. Retrieved 19 August 2017 from www.education.gov.au/australian-maths-and-science-partnerships-programme-amspp.

Boaler, J. (1997). *Experiencing School Mathematics—teaching styles, sex and setting.* Buckingham: Open University Press.

Breiner, J. M., Johnson, C. C., Harkness, S. S., & Koelher, C. M. (2012). 'What is STEM? A discussion about conceptions of STEM in education and partnerships'. *School Science and Mathematics*, 112(1), pp. 3–11.

Butin, D. W. (2003). 'Of what use is it? Multiple conceptualizations of service learning within education'. *Teachers College Record*, 105(9), pp. 1674–92.

Bybee, R. W. (1997). *Achieving scientific literacy: From purposes to practical action.* Portsmouth, NH: Heinemann.

Campbell, C., & Chittleborough, G. (2014). 'The "new" science specialists: Promoting and improving the teaching of science in primary schools'. *Teaching Science,* 60(1) pp. 19–29.

Chesebrough, D. (1994). 'Informal science teacher preparation'. *Science Education International*, 5(2), pp. 28–33.

Chinnapan, M., Dinham, S., Herrington, T. & Scott, D. (2007). 'Year 12 students and Higher Mathematics: Emerging issues'. Refereed conference proceedings, AARE Annual Conference.

Clarke, D. (2016). Paper presented at the Reconceptualising Mathematics and Science Teacher Education Programs (ReMSTEP) Conference, Melbourne. (unpublished).

Clarke, D. J. (2013). 'Contingent Conceptions of Accomplished Practice: The Cultural Specificity of Discourse in and about the Mathematics Classroom', *ZDM: The International Journal in Mathematics Education*, 45(1), pp. 21–33.

Clarke, D. & Hollingsworth H. (2002) 'Elaborating a model of teacher professional growth', *Teaching and Teacher Education*,18(8), pp. 947–67, Nov. 2002., p. 957.

Cobb, P. (2000). 'The importance of a situated view of learning to the design of research and instruction'. In Boaler, J. (Ed.), *Multiple perspectives on mathematics and teaching and learning.* Westport, CT: Greenwood Publishing Group, Inc.

Cobern, W. W. & Loving, C. C. (1998). 'The card activity: Introducing teachers to the philosophy of science'. In W. McComas (Ed.), *The nature of science in science education: Rationales and strategies* (pp. 73–82). Dordrecht, Netherlands: Kluwer Academic Publishers.

Committee for the Review of Teaching and Teacher Education. (2003). 'Australia's Teachers: Australia's Future Advancing Innovation, Science, Technology and Mathematics', Main Report. Canberra: DEST.

Corrigan, D. (2015). Five levels of cognitive engagement. Personal communication (March).

Curtis, D. J., Howden, M., Curtis, F., McColm, I., Scrine, J., Blomfield, T., Reeve, I., & Ryan, T. (2014). 'Drama and environment: Joining forces to engage children and young people in environmental education'. *Australian Journal of Environmental Education*, 29(2), pp. 182–201.

Darby, L. (2005). 'Science students' perceptions of engaging pedagogy'. *Research in Science Education*, 35(4), pp. 425–45.

Dawborn-Gundlach, M., Pesina, J, Rochette, E., Hubber, P., Gaff, P., Henry, D., Gibson, M., Kelly, L., Redman, C., (2017). 'Enhancing preservice concepts of earth science through an immersion, conceptual museum learning program (Reconceptualising rocks)'. *Teaching and Teacher Education*. 67, pp. 214–26.

Dinham, S. (2007). 'Specialist Primary Teachers: Experts in the field', ACER, available at: www.researchgate.net/publication/265619917_Specialist_primary_teachers_Experts_in_the_field.

Dinham, S. (2014). 'Primary Schooling in Australia: Pseudo-Science Plus Extras Times Growing Inequality Equals Decline'. In 'What Counts as Quality in Education?' Refereed Conference Proceedings ACE 2014 National Conference. Carlton South, Victoria: Australian College of Educators, pp. 8–15. Available at: www.austcolled.com.au/documents/item/80.

Dinham, S. (2015). 'Opening Address', ReMSTEP Annual Conference, Melbourne, 13th November. http://remstep.org.au/conference/conference-archive.html.

Dinham, S. (2016). *Leading Learning and Teaching*. Melbourne, ACER Press.

Dinham, S. (2017). 'Reconceptualising mathematics and science teacher education programs. Final report'. Canberra, ACT: Australian Government Department of Education and Training.

Dweck, C. (2000). *Self-Theories—Their Role in Motivation, Personality and Development*. Philadelphia, PA: Psychology Press.

Edwards, D., Perkins, K., Pearce, J. and Hong J. (2015). *Work Integrated Learning in STEM in Australian Universities*. Australian Council for Educational Research (ACER).

English, L. D. (2016). Targeting all of STEM in the primary school: Engineering design as a foundational process. Proceedings of the ACER Research Conference: Improving STEM learning: What will it take? pp. 84–88. Camberwell: Australian Council for Educational Research (ACER).

Fennema, E., & Franke, M. L. (1992). 'Teachers' knowledge and its impact'. In Grouws, D. A. (Ed.), *Handbook of research on mathematics teaching and learning: A project of the National Council of Teachers of Mathematics*. pp. 147–64. New York: Macmillan

Freely Accessible Remote Laboratories (FARLabs) (n.d.). Retrieved 19 August 19 2017 from www.farlabs.edu.au.

Freeman, B., Marginson, S., & Tytler, R. (2015). *The age of STEM:*

Educational policy and practice across the world in science, technology, engineering and mathematics. London: Routledge.

Frykholm, J., & Glasson, G. (2005). 'Connecting Mathematics and Science Instruction: Pedagogical Context Knowledge for Teachers'. *School Science and Mathematics*, 105(3), pp. 127–41.

Galbraith, P. (2006a). 'Real world problems: Developing principles of design'. In Grootenboer, P., Zevenbergen, R. & Chinnappan, M. (Eds.), *Identities cultures and learning spaces* (Vol. 1). Canberra, ACT: Mathematical Education Research Group of Australasia.

Galbraith, P. (2006b). 'Students, mathematics, and technology: assessing the present—challenging the future'. *International Journal of Mathematical Education in Science and Technology*, 37(3), pp. 277–90, Apr. 2006.

Galbraith, P., Stillman, G., & Brown, J. (2006). 'Identifying key transition activities for enhanced engagement in mathematical modelling'. In Grootenboer, P., Zevenbergen, R., & Chinnappan, M. (Eds.), *Identities cultures and learning spaces* (Vol. 1). Canberra, ACT: Mathematical Education Research Group of Australasia.

GCA (2015). *The Australian Graduate Survey Report 2014*. Graduate Careers Australia, Melbourne. Accessed Oct 8 2015 from www.graduatecareers.com.au/research/researchreports.

Goodrum, D., Hackling, M., & Rennie, L. J. (2001). *The status and quality of teaching and learning of science in Australian schools*. Canberra: Australian Department of Education Science and Training.

Growing Tall Poppies (n.d.). Retrieved 19 August 2017 from www.growingtallpoppies.com.

Hackling, M., Murcia, K., West, J., & Anderson, K. (2013). 'Optimising STEM Education in WA Schools, Part 1: Summary Report'. Edith Cowan Institute for Education. Retrieved from http://www.tiac.wa.gov.au/Files/STEM_Report_Part-1_20022014.aspx.

Hobbs, L. (2012). 'Teaching "out-of-field" as a boundary-crossing event', *International Journal of Mathematics and Science Education*, 11(2), pp. 1–31.

Honey, M., Pearson, G., & Schweingruber, H. (2014). *STEM Integration* in *K–12 Education: Status, Prospects, and an Agenda for Research*. Washington, D.C.: National Academies Press.

Howard, P., & Perry B. (2007). A school-community model for enhancing Aboriginal students' mathematical learning. 'Mathematics: Essential research, essential practice'. Proceedings of the 30th annual conference of the Mathematics Education Research Group of Australasia, Hobart.

Hubber, P, Tytler, R., & Haslam, F. (2010). 'Teaching and learning about force with a representational focus: Pedagogy and teacher change', *Research in Science Education*, 40(1), 5–28.

In2science (n.d.). Retrieved 19 August 2017 from https://In2science.org.au.

In2science (2017). 'In2science science and maths peer mentoring in schools'. Accessed 15 May 2017 from www.in2science.org.au.

Jones, M., Hobbs, L., Kenny, J., Campbell, C., Chittleborough, G., Gilbert, A., Herbert, S., & Redman, C. (2016). 'Successful university-school partnerships: An interpretive framework to inform partnership practice'. *Teaching and Teacher Education*, 60:108–20.

Jung, M. L., & Tonso, K. L. (2006). 'Elementary preservice teachers learning to teach science in science museums and nature centers: A novel program's impact on science knowledge, science pedagogy, and confidence teaching'. *Journal of Elementary Science Education*, 18(1), pp. 15–31.

Kennepohl, D., Baran, J., Connors, M., Quigley, K., & Currie, R. (2006). 'Remote Access to Instrumental Analysis for Distance Education in Science'. *The International Review of Research in Open and Distributed Learning*, 6(3). Retrieved from www.irrodl.org/index.php/irrodl/article/view/260.

Kruger, T., Davies, A., Eckersley, B., Newell, F., & Cherednichenko, B., (2009). *Effective and sustainable university-school partnerships. Beyond determined efforts of inspired individuals.* Canberra: Teaching Australia [Electronic version]. Retrieved from http://hdl.voced.edu.au/10707/144200.

Latour, B. (1986). 'Visualization and cognition: Drawing things together'. *Knowledge and Society*, 6, pp. 1–40.

Lederman, N. G. (1999). 'Teachers' understanding of the nature of science and classroom practice: Factors that facilitate or impede the relationship'. *Journal of Research in Science Teaching*, 36(8), pp. 916–29.

Lehrer, R., & Schauble, L. (2000). *Modeling in mathematics and science. Advances in instructional psychology.* Mahwah, NJ: Lawrence Erlbaum Associates, pp. 101–05.

Lehrer, R., & Schauble, L. (2012). 'Seeding evolutionary thinking by engaging children in modeling its foundations'. *Science Education*, 96(4), pp. 701–24.

Lindahl, B. (2007). 'A longitudinal study of students' attitudes towards science and choice of career'. In 80th NARST International Conference. New Orleans, Louisiana.

Loughran, J. & Smith, K. (2015). 'Facilitating change in science teachers' perceptions about learning and teaching'. In D. Corrigan, C. Buntting, J. Dillon, A. Jones & R. Gunstone, (Eds.), *The Future in Learning Science: What's in it for the Learner?* Dordrecht: Springer, pp. 279–94.

Lyons, T. (2006a). 'Different countries, same science classes: Students' experiences of school science in their own words'. *International Journal of Science Education,* 28(6), pp. 591–613.

Lyons, T. (2006b). 'The puzzle of falling enrolments in physics and chemistry courses: Putting some pieces together'. *Research in Science Education*, 36(3), pp. 285–311.

Marginson, S., Tytler, R., Freeman, B., & Roberts, K. (2013). 'STEM: Country comparisons'. Melbourne: The Australian Council of Learned Academies. www.acola.org.au.

McKinnon, M. & Lamberts, R. (2014). 'Influencing science teaching self-efficacy beliefs of primary school teachers: A longitudinal case study'. *International Journal of Science Education*, Part B 4(2) pp. 172–94.

Nardi, E., & Steward, S. (2003). 'Is mathematics T.I.R.E.D? A profile of quiet disaffection in secondary mathematics classrooms'. *British Educational Research Journal*, 29, pp. 345–66.

National Council (2015). National STEM School Education Strategy,

2016–2026. Retrieved http://www.educationcouncil.edu.au/site/DefaultSite/filesystem/documents/National%20STEM%20School%20Education%20Strategy.pdf.

National Curriculum Board, (May 2009). *Shape of the Australian Curriculum: Mathematics*, p. 5, © Commonwealth of Australia 2017.

Office of the Chief Scientist (2012a). 'Health of Australian Science'. Canberra: Australian Government.

Office of the Chief Scientist (2012b). 'Mathematics, engineering and science in the national interest'. Canberra: Commonwealth of Australia. Retrieved from www.chiefscientist.gov.au/wp-content/uploads/Office-of-the-Chief-Scientist-MES-Report-8-May-2012.pdf.

Office of the Chief Scientist (2014). Science, Technology, Engineering and Mathematics: Australia's Future. Canberra: Commonwealth of Australia. Retrieved from http://www.chiefscientist.gov.au/wp-content/uploads/STEM_AustraliasFuture_Sept2014_Web.pdf.

Office of the Chief Scientist (2016a). STEM Programme Index. www.chiefscientist.gov.au/2016/01/spi-2016-stem-programme-index-2016-2/

Office of the Chief Scientist (2016b). 'Australia's STEM workforce: Science, technology, engineering and mathematics'. Canberra: Commonwealth of Australia.

Osborne, J., & Collins, S. (2001). 'Pupils' views of the role and value of the science curriculum: A focus group study'. International Journal of Science Education, 23(5), pp. 441–67.

Paris, S. G. (1997). 'Situated motivation and informal learning'. *Journal of Museum Education*, 22, pp. 22–27.

Prain, V., & Tytler, R. (2012). 'Learning through constructing representations in science: A framework of representational construction affordances'. *International Journal of Science Education*, 34(17), pp. 2751–73.

Productivity Commission (2012). 'Schools Workforce Research Report'. Canberra: Productivity Commission. (p. 90)

Prinsley, R. and Baranyai, K. (2015). 'STEM skills in the Workforce: What do employers want?' Office of the Chief Scientist of Australia,

Occasional Paper Series, 9 Mar. Accessed 20 October 2015 from www.chiefscientist.gov.au/wp-content/uploads/OPS09_02Mar2015_Web.pdf.

Rennie, L., (2007). 'Values in science portrayed in out-of-school contexts'. In Corrigan D., Dillon J. & Gunstone R., (Eds.). *The Re-Emergence of Values in Science Education*. Rotterdam: Sense Publishers, pp. 197–212.

Richmond, G., Dershimer, R. C., Ferreira, M., Maylone, N., Kubitskey, B. & Meriweather, A. (2017). 'Developing and sustaining an educative mentoring model of STEM teacher professional development through collaborative partnership'. *Mentoring and Tutoring: Partnership in learning* 25(1) pp. 5–26.

Stacey, K. (2010). Mathematical and scientific literacy around the world. *Journal of Mathematics and Science Education in Southeast Asia*, 33(1), pp. 1–16.

Stuckey, M., Hofstein, A., Mamlok-Naaman, R. & Eilks, I. (2013). 'The meaning of "relevance" in science education and its implications for the science curriculum'. *Studies in Science Education*, 49(1), p. 1034.

Sullivan, P. (2011). 'Teaching Mathematics: Using research-informed strategies'. *Australian Educational Review* (59).

Taylor, A. R., Jones, M. G., Broadwell, B., & Oppewal, T. (2008). 'Creativity, inquiry or accountability? Scientists' and teachers' perceptions of science education'. *Science Education*, 92(6), pp. 1058–1075. https://doi.org/10.1002/sce.20272.

Thomson, S., De Bortoli, L. & Underwood, C. (2016). *PISA 2015: A first look at Australia's Results*. Australian Council for Educational Research. Retrieved from: http://research.acer.edu.au/cgi/viewcontent.cgi?article=1021&context=ozpisa.

Thomson, S., Wernert, N., O'Grady, E. & Rodrigues, S. (2016). '*TIMSS 2015: A first look at Australia's Results*'. Australian Council for Educational Research. Retrieved from: https://research.acer.edu.au/timss_2015/1/.

Tytler, R. (2007). 'Re-imagining science education: Engaging students in science for Australia's future'. *Australian Educational Review*, 51.

Melbourne: ACER. Retrieved from http://research.acer.edu.au/aer/3/.

Tytler, R. (2010). 'Ways forward for primary science education: A review commissioned by the Swedish National Agency for Education'.

Tytler, R. (2014). 'Attitudes, Identity and Aspirations toward Science'. In Lederman, N. G. & Abell, S. K. (Eds), *Handbook of Science Education*, Volume II pp. 82–103. New York: Routledge.

Tytler, R. & Osborne, J. (2012). 'Student attitudes and aspirations towards science'. In B. Fraser, K. Tobin, & C. McRobbie (Eds.) *Second International Handbook of Science Education*, pp. 597-625. Dordrecht, Netherlands: Springer.

Tytler, R., Symington, D., & Cripps Clark, J. (2016). 'Community-school collaborations in science: Towards improved outcomes through better understanding of boundary issues'. *International Journal of Mathematics and Science Education* (DOI: 10.1007/s10763-015-9711-9).

Tytler, R., Symington, D., Kirkwood, V., & Malcolm, C. (2008). 'Engaging students in authentic science through school–community links: learning from the rural experience'. *Teaching Science, the Journal of the Australian Science Teachers Association*, 54(3), pp. 13–8.

Tytler, R., Symington, D., & Smith, C. (2011). 'A curriculum innovation framework for science, technology and mathematics education'. *Research in Science Education*, 41, pp. 19–38.

Tytler, R., Symington, D., Williams, G., White, P., Campbell, C., Chittleborough, G., Upstill, G., Roper, E., & Dziadkiewicz N., (2015). 'Building productive partnerships for STEM Education: Evaluating the model and outcomes of the Scientists and Mathematicians in Schools program'. Melbourne: Deakin University. Available at: https://www.csiro.au/~/media/Education-media/Files/STEM-Prof-Schools/Productive-Partnerships-STEM-Education-PDF.pdf?la=en&hash=32DC08424BB8C1BF9614123CEBF040F064E23DE0

Tytler, R., Osborne, J., Williams, G., Tytler, K., & Cripps Clark, J. (2008). 'Opening up pathways: Engagement in STEM across the Primary-Secondary school transition'. Canberra: Australian Department of Education, Employment and Workplace Relations. Retrieved from http://pandora.nla.gov.au/tep/88047.

Tytler, R., Prain, V., Hubber, P., & Waldrip, B. (Eds.). (2013). *Constructing representations to learn in science*. Rotterdam, The Netherlands: Sense Publishers.

Tytler, R., & Symington, D (2006). 'Science in school and society'. *Teaching Science*, 52(3), pp. 10–15.

Vasquez, J. (2015). STEM: 'Beyond the acronym'. *Educational Leadership*, pp. 11–15.

Victorian Curriculum and Assessment Authority (VCAA) (2015). Victorian Certificate of Education Biology Study Design. Accreditation Period Unit 1 and 2 2016–2020 and Unit 3 and 4 2017–2021.

Weldon, Paul R. (2016). 'Out-of-field teaching in Australian secondary schools'. *Policy Insights*, (6). Melbourne: Australian Council for Educational Research (ACER).

Wood, T., Williams, G., & Mc Neal, B. (2006). 'Children's mathematical thinking in different classroom cultures'. *Journal for Research in Mathematics Education*, 37 (3), pp. 222–52.

www.ingramcontent.com/pod-product-compliance
Lightning Source LLC
Chambersburg PA
CBHW052024070526
44584CB00016B/1884